HOW ON EARTH?

A Reflection On
Thirty Years of European
Music and Art Tours

ROMA RANDLES

Published by Silverbird Publishing Pty Ltd
Address: PO Box72, Eltham, Victoria 3095

First published in Australia 2021
This edition published 2021
Copyright © Roma Randles 2021

ISBN: 978-0-6450296-8-0

Cover design, typesetting: WorkingType (www.workingtype.com.au)

The right of Roma Randles to be identified as the Author of the Work has been asserted in accordance with the Copyright, Designs and Patents Act 1988. The Author of this book accepts all responsibility for the contents and absolves any other person or persons involved in its production from any responsibility or liability where the contents are concerned.

All rights reserved. No part of this publication may be reproduced, stored in a retrieval system, or transmitted, in any form or by any means without the prior written permission of the publisher, nor be otherwise circulated in any form of binding or cover other than that in which it is published and without a similar condition being imposed on the subsequent purchaser.

Most of the names mentioned in this memoir are true.
Just occasionally fictitious ones have been used

Randles, Roma
How on Earth? A Covid Reflection On Thirty Years of European Tours
pp206

*For All My Children and
All My Grandchildren*

With Love.

"The most blessed and privileged of all callings is that of the musician, who acts as interpreter, inspirer, teacher, healer, consoler and above all, as a humble servant…"
— Yehudi Menuhin

FROM AN INFORMATION PAGE ON ROMA'S TOURS

LINGUA MUSICA was registered in Melbourne in 1987 and is under the directorship of ROMA RANDLES, who has combined a long career in Music Performance. (both in the solo and chamber music sphere) and Teaching... (Pianoforte as well as History and Literature of Music) with the demands of raising a large family and being-the busy wife of a professional man. Perhaps her undoubted organising skills stem from these diverse life roles.

Roma Randles pursued her own career both in Australia and during the eight years the family lived in England, as well as undertaking some post graduate study in London. Her teaching experience has been at the senior level in both countries. Many of her former students are themselves today following musical careers.

During the eighties, Roma began to diversify these interests into some more managerial roles .... organising concerts, master classes, private courses for adults, arranging music weekends, and also organising and managing Australian tours for some overseas artists.

It was during this time that she was approached about the idea of creating and conducting European tours. At first she was reluctant to do this, but persuaded by UTA French Airlines, she finally agreed, and the LINGUA MUSICA annual Music /Arts Tours were born!

They have been an enormous effort, but have now become quite established on the Australian travel scene, with people from all over the country returning again and again to join her on these exciting European adventures.

Roma Randles makes all the arrangements, in conjunction with her Australian agent and all her European ones, as well as her very well known private contacts in Europe. She invites distinguished lecturers and performers at the top of their fields, and who are often personal friends, to be associated with the tours. This is one of the many aspects which make the LINGUA MUSICA tours so unique. On tour as well, she acts as Tour Manager and Cultural Adviser, gives some lectures in her own field, and just occasionally performs for her group.

The tours are expertly organised, and no detail is too small for her constant attention. Variety is a well considered keynote, and so much varied content is included which brings great vitality to every tour. Learning-whilst-travelling is another concept Roma holds dear, and this is a major aspect of every LINGUA MUSICA tour.

Of course necessary free time for rest, contemplation, and independent discovery are important on tour too, and these times are built in to every programme.

Whilst discovering many different corners of Europe, wonderful excursions, great architecture, history, art, food and wines, and above all, great music, simple fun is an element never forgotten. Many new and long lasting friendships have been forged during a LINGUA MUSICA Tour.

CONTENTS

From An Information Page On Roma's Tours	vii
Introduction	xiii
And So To Begin!	1
"How On Earth?"	7
"Aldeburgh And Beyond"	17
Celebrating Mozart Tour	27
Ruth Nye, MBE. FRCM	41
"Great Music Houses Of Europe"	48
"Anniversaries And More"	56
"You Must Be Joking! Alas No…"	59
Reflections:	76
The Menuhin Festival Gstaad	78
Triumphant Opening of Yehudi Menuhin Memorial Hall	81
Leipzig And Weimar	84
Music Helps Heal Holocaust Wounds?	89
"Our Russian Tours"	94
St Petersburg	99
Scandinavia	121
2001 "A French/Italian Rhapsody"	128
"A Feast Of Wine And Music"	135
"2007…A Tour With a Difference"	140
Vienna Boys' Choir	147
"Liszt Bicentenary and More"	149
Further Moments Recalled	155

Some Further Tour Locations 158
Angela Hewitt and the Trasimeno Festivals 164
"Two Festivals Tour" 168
Composers' Houses: 174
"A Spanish Rhapsody" 178
Conclusion 188
Acknowledgements 190

FOREWORD
CHRISTOPER BARNES, AM

I have been lucky to have had a few teachers who have influenced my love and appreciation of Music, and one of these was Roma Randles, the other was my father. I was conscious of good music from a very early age, having been born in Edward Elgar country in Herefordshire. In fact my family has several connections to Elgar.

And so, half a world away in 1999, I joined one of Roma's LINGUA MUSICA tours. It was filled with many great moments, amongst which, on the first of my tours with her, we attended the International Chopin Piano Festival in the beautiful spa town of Duszniki in S/W Poland. Here I learned of Roma's undoubted organising skills. By then, she had organised the group, arranged pre-tour meetings, visited all the tour destinations, flown us to Prague with Lauda Air, coached us to Duszniki, with a typically Russian four hour wait at the Czech border where the guards tried unsuccessfully to extract more money from her, and had us booked into the best hotel in Duszniki in time for dinner before the concert.

The Chopin was memorable and with soloists like Nikolai Demidenko (who I was to hear later so often in London, Paris, Sydney etc) and the eminent Piers lane, who insisted on sitting with Roma, so we knew we were in good company.

So many other great experiences with LINGUA MUSICA over the following years. There were some personal characteristics about the L/M tours which were of Roma's making. The groups are all of a type and we all enjoy one another's company. We are here to learn more about music and the wonderful destinations we visit. My memories of Rostropovich playing the Shoshtokovitch 'Cello Concerto in the vast Marquee in Gstaad, Switzerland, our amazing visit to Weimar and hearing the Israel Philharmonic under Zubin Mehta perform the great Mahler Symphony No 2, in Ljubljana, a wonderful performance by a Piano Trio in the castle, various performances of famous Ruth Nye, especially one in Nohant, near the home of Chopin and his lover George Sand. Another highlight was in Baden-Baden, at the Festspielhaus, hearing the great Beethoven 5th from the Berlin Philharmonic, under Sir Simon Rattle.

Perhaps the most remarkable performance was in the palatial Hotel Negresco, Nice, when the guest pianist failed to appear. Not to be deterred, Roma sat down and amazed us by playing some immaculate Liszt and Chopin polonaises and a ballade.

The highlights were not only musical. I remember the exquisite gardens of the Villa Ephrussi de Rothschild at Cap Ferrat, beautiful St Paul de Vence, the magnificent St Thomas Church of Bach fame in Leipzig; and visits to Venice and Prague, were unique experiences.

Roma has, over the years, on her LINGA MUSICA tours, educated dozens of new music lovers, and given us all great pleasure. Thank you Roma.

INTRODUCTION

The long COVID 19 lockdown in Melbourne has at times seemed endless. Interestingly though, it would appear that many have used this solitary time for some creative efforts of diverse kinds. Many remarkable stories and projects have emerged. One or two of these prompted me finally to do what I have been urged by so many friends to do for years… to write an account of the thirty years of European Music and Art tours, which I had personally created and led.

As a professional musician of long standing, and a busy wife and mother of a large family, I suppose it does sound a fairly unlikely thing to have accomplished. But with all this unusual time on my hands and browsing through my many years of personal travel diaries, I have come to the conclusion that it is a story which could be of some interest. It did indeed happen! Thirty years of very full and remarkable tours to so many different parts of Europe, with experience of great music, great musicians, and great art in great locations. Yes. I now finally agree with all those who have been requesting it for years. It's a great story. But where to begin? How did it happen? That's now my challenge.

Memories of the events I will write about remain clear. But forgive me if on occasion, the description of an event in a certain tour actually happened on a previous or a following one.

AND SO TO BEGIN!

Where to begin? How to begin? I think back to my first book, "A LIFE IN MUSIC...Ruth Nye and the Arrau Heritage", which was published in London in 2012. Though the included tour events described at the beginning of this book happened in 1999, a truly remarkable year of important international anniversaries (for which I organised a very successful "Anniversaries and More" tour), they have inspired me to write more about the kind of experiences my beloved tour members have enjoyed with me during some thirty years of annual LINGUA MUSICA European Music and Art tours.

Even as I write that number, I find myself rather stunned. How on earth? How did it ever happen? Where did it start? Was I mad? How could I, on my own, ever have created such a thing? How to describe me....a sole operator? A one man band? A risk-taker? Over-confident? No...certainly not that. Originally, I was never full of confidence...the opposite in fact. Much knowledge and experience of Music, a fairly extensive knowledge of Europe....but absolutely NO knowledge whatsoever of how to create and put securely in place the hundreds of components of an extensive European tour. These include all the route choices, means of travel, accommodation, performances (both major ones and private), meals, lectures, guests, guides, art experts and galleries, excursions, drivers, and more. And then to **guarantee** to those prepared to join me (and to pay for such a tour) that everything outlined in their brochures would indeed happen. Even now, as I ponder all this, I feel a belated shiver of apprehension. But the amazing thing is that yes...that first tour did work beautifully. It required so much solitary effort beforehand, it required 'going out on a limb' a little....deposits did not cover everything and one had to trust that the balance would. It did. Endless telephone calls, at first not even a fax machine (quickly acquired) let alone a computer (did we have computers then?) But finally, LINGUA MUSICA, was indeed officially registered with the Department of Business Affairs, and became a going concern.

It is August 16th as I start to put my thoughts about the tours together and suddenly I remember that in just four months' time, December 16th 2020, we will be celebrating the actual 250th birthday of Ludwig van Beethoven! In fact this entire year is one of remembrance and celebration of this remarkable genius who was born at 3.40 am on that day in 1770 in the city of Bonn, West Germany, and died in 1827, when the lines following his coffin in Vienna were extraordinary. He remains perhaps the most revered composer of all time. His compositions include 32 sonatas covering every facet of a pianist's skill, 9 symphonies, 5 piano concertos, 1 violin concerto, a triple concerto, the opera, 'Fidelio', violin and cello sonatas, piano trios, string quartets, Masses....and more, much more. The entire world celebrates Beethoven this year, and in particular, Germany has endless concerts with the greatest living musicians, exhibitions, opera, films, dance and theatre...all to celebrate Germany's revered historic musical master. There are no less than 300 projects arranged. He was a humanist, a maverick, a musical visionary, and a great lover of Nature. Even his deafness which first began to plague him as early as his late twenties failed to stop his creative impulse. My own love of the music of Beethoven is unquestionable. I studied and played a great deal of it. I never did an actual Beethoven Tour. But he was always there...always a major feature of so many concerts, opera and lectures on my adventures.

The first tour I had put together was advertised. I prepared colourfully illustrated and detailed brochures. I spent hours copying materials at Officeworks. Very often my family were quite bemused. Daughter, Jackie, remarked to some friends, "When Mum speaks about 'cutting and pasting' she's actually talking about scissors and a glu-stick!" Well, for heaven's sake, I was a professional musician....what did I know about on-line 'cutting and pasting'! The content was the important thing and people seemed to like it. Then people began to book...they actually **booked**! The anticipated first tour was off and running with a lovely little signed up group of nine. I was so happy as the family saw me off to fly ahead with UTA French Airlines, but also full of apprehension. Will everything be ok? Will it be a disaster? (A glass of bubbly here and there en route did help restore confidence...well, a bit). But it was a **success!** It was wonderful! There were indeed some hiccups along the way on that first tour...sometimes hilarious ones...some not quite so. However, my never- veered- from rule right from the start, had always been that before meeting a group at the designated venue, I visit every tour location and personally check that every 'on- tour' detail is in place. This has been an enormous additional effort as you may imagine, but has ensured there is always a workable solution to any unexpected problem which might arise.

My great joy in Music, my involvement with great Music whenever possible for so many years...all my life really...was the overriding factor in agreeing to create and conduct these tours. Music had delighted and sometimes overwhelmed me from the time I was a tiny tot. In the evenings, my parents used to listen to classical music on their old records or on the wireless, and I, tucked up in bed and supposed to be asleep, would listen in. One of my mother's obvious favourites, Nellie Melba singing "Hark, hear the gentle lark" was played so often I eventually knew the words by heart. I remember also being slightly alarmed by Melba's dramatic rendition of what I was later told was the "Queen of the Night" aria and pulling the blanket over my head! My own advances in Music were always greatly encouraged, through Primary, Secondary and Tertiary levels and they were so delighted when various scholarships and bursaries were awarded. Later of course, in our own home, Music was alive and well. One could truly claim it was "A house full of Music". Someone always practising (violin, piano, clarinet, guitar, recorder), piano lessons, rehearsals of chamber music, wonderful recordings...and even to the extent of a very early -rising husband who at 6am might be happily listening as he made the toast and waited for the kettle to boil, if the music emerging from the little kitchen radio happened to be opera... often to howls of protest from above!

So MUSIC....it was always there and I was always happy sharing this overwhelming love with others, with those who already had knowledge of classical music, and to help enlighten those who did not, firstly through teaching, then my concerts and later when I was persuaded to create my tours, through simple lectures about form and relationships in the works they would hear, and of course, the history which surrounded them. Music does not exist in a vacuum. My idea later became to combine all this with visiting the most marvellous European cities associated with that music, great architecture, great art galleries, great food and wine and other magnificent and significant inclusions along the way. Quite a challenge! But of course, originally I never dreamed any such thing could happen.

My tours were never designed to make money...they were carefully designed to cover all costs including my own, and possibly there might be something left over! I was never in the financial position to have been able to travel abroad every year. (Of course as the numbers increased, some profit was made, but never very much because the content was so extensive.) But these tours made it possible for me to experience that annual European travel. More importantly, they increased my learning and understanding at every turn. They have also given me the greatest joy, sense of fulfilment and personal confidence. It appears such experiences have also brought great joy and greatly valued new knowledge and friendship to so many people, who have written wonderful appreciative accounts, and many who have returned to travel with me four and even five times. I have also met many distinguished personalities along the way, some of whom I will tell you about later.

The success of that first tour (planned as a probable 'one-off') gave me the confidence to continue to offer annual ones. Each has been different; different locations, from North to South, (St Petersburg to Sicily), and East to West, (Budapest to Bordeaux) in Europe, the UK and one to

Ireland. Major European Music Festivals featured greatly in the designs, as did little known smaller but brilliant festivals in superb locations, such as those in Poland and Italy. The European Union also used to name certain cities each year as being that year's "Cultural Capital", and this fact too figured in my plans. Sometimes the outlines overlapped, and one particular tour, "**Great European Houses of Music**" was so popular it was repeated twice, with a little variation each time.

That 'one off' in 1989 was actually the first of thirty wonderful L/M European tours ending with "A Spanish Rhapsody" in 2017. (During a couple of those years there were actually two tours). All were given titles. It was much fun considering what to name each. This very long **COVID 19** isolation time in Melbourne has been absolutely unnerving and bewildering, but surprisingly, there have been unexpected positives as well. The enforced isolation has given me time to reflect a great deal, to remember so much, and to write an account of our musical adventures and, very importantly, the life circumstances which led up to their creation. This incredible pandemic has also caused the postponement of European tours and international travel of all kinds. When the world returns to normal, LINGUA MUSICA will again provide richness of experience, with perhaps a slightly different touch under its new Director; but always with the professionalism, creativity, aims, and personal attention which have been its hallmarks for so many years.

It would be totally beyond the pale to set out to write a full descript of every single one of the thirty tours and am sure would actually be unwelcome. I have chosen to describe a few in quite some detail, others, though equally as important, a little less so. Then highlights, great personalities encountered, great music experienced in great locations, points of difference, fresh ideas, incredible happenings, comedies, tragedies (well, almost on occasion) and above all, great friendships created. And lastly, but by no means least, always a great deal of fun combined with our sometime sense of awe.

Just some of the LINGUA MUSICA European Music and Art tours...(Not in any particular order)

"ALDEBURGH AND BEYOND"

"CELEBRATING MOZART TOUR"

"MOSTLY EASTERN AND RUSSIA TOO!"

"MOSTLY FRENCH AND MORE"

"ANNIVERSARIES AND MORE"

"A FRENCH/ITALIAN RHAPSODY"

"GREAT EUROPEAN HOUSES OF MUSIC"
(repeated twice)

"MUSIC FESTIVALS OF GSTAAD AND SALZBURG"

"A NORTH / SOUTH ODYSSEY"

"ANOTHER NORTH / SOUTH ODYSSEY"

"SUMMER FESTIVALS PLUS"

"A FEAST OF WINE AND MUSIC"

"MUSIC, MOUNTAINS, MAGIC AND MORE"

"THE LISZT BICENTENNARY AND MORE"

"SWISS MUSIC FESTIVALS"

"A SPANISH RHAPSODY"

"HOW ON EARTH?"

The immediate task I have set myself is to TRY to remember how it all came about.

We returned to Australia at the very end of 1981, after spending eight years living in England (during two different periods, fitting in with our childrens' secondary education, early 1961–1966 and again, 1979– end of 1981). During the earlier period, my husband was the Dentist for the Corporation of the City of London, with his surgery attached to The Mansion House, home of the Lord Mayor of London, and just around the corner from 'The Old Lady of Threadneedle Street'. We got to know so well and to love the winding streets and alleys of this ancient square mile which constitutes the City of London. Seeing the stripe-panted straight- backed fellows with their black furled umbrellas and leather brief cases returning from the leading business houses of the world always intrigued me. So much intrigued me. Such a remarkable space. The building of The Mansion House with its Palladian facade, had commenced in 1739, and its special gold and white Egyptian Hall was the setting for the Lord and Lady Mayoress's receptions. They even used to give a Children's Christmas party here each year, to which those of our little ones old enough to attend were invited. With my au pair holding the fort, and after a long afternoon session with Prof. Urquart, I sometimes met my husband near there, or at Monument, or nearer Christopher Wren's masterpiece, St Paul's Cathedral, after he had finished surgery, and we would look for a little bar or restaurant. Still in my mid-twenties, and having never left Australia, I had known very little of all this and was always so anxious to read and learn more. I remember with gentle amusement once when Kevin had had a particularly busy day in the surgery, his sitting down, raising his glass with that gorgeous smile and bidding me "Good Rinse!" Obviously it was time that evening for a restful dinner! We would discuss our respective days, feel anew how fortunate we were to be here, and perhaps giggle over some ridiculous aspect of our new life, including the still rigid boundaries of the class system. "So unlike in Australia" (or were we kidding ourselves just a little?). Then possibly a concert at the Festival Hall or a theatre in the West End. We adored it all.

Kevin just loved his work in the City, running a busy practice with absolutely everything provided for him and getting to know so many of his patients, including members of the City Police (not to be confused with 'The Met', the different force in the West End.) Years later, when we were leaving, the President of an organisation to which he belonged wrote that Kevin had been "like a breath of Spring". We pondered that. Kevin had always been immaculately dressed in his full whites, and completely dignified as his prestigious role demanded, but he also brought to the job, a complete absence of that "uptightness" (if there is such a word) and instead, an open, laughing, friendly, interested Australian attitude... obviously welcomed all round.

But on another front, life was extremely busy with a very young family, much hard work, studying, and running a large old leased house on the border of London/Kent, "Victoriana at its very worst", I used to claim. But it was also wonderfully roomy and comfortable and with a small pretty walled garden, just large enough for swing, slide etc. and masses of roses, both climbing and otherwise. A lot of work but became a great family home for us. During these times of little children (early school and kindergarten), I had also been very busy musically, studying, and teaching (during the second period in England, I had actually taught at the former school of Dame Myra Hess). And as well travelling quite often with our family, both around the UK, (including Scotland and Wales) and in Europe. No luxury tours these; we had bought our own caravan! A most wonderful education for our children, and for us all. My husband and I also took the very occasional short European trip alone for various cultural experiences and/or to visit friends...especially in France and Spain. One could say, we developed a great love for and knowledge of Europe through these travels, and of course our life in London and later in Marlow-on-Thames, offered the very best opportunities for music, art and theatre (my husband's passion) as well as my own on-going musical studies, teaching and very occasional small performances.

Back in Melbourne, I was very busy indeed. Running a household, all the childrens' activities, school committees, gardening, entertaining very occasionally, two of my large family still at school, others at University. Performing a little, accompanying a lot, playing orchestral reductions for students' concerto performances (terrible things these...never meant to fit easily under a pianist's hands), and teaching" History and Literature of Music "at Year Twelve level, which I loved because my greatest interest in that field was 'Form and Analysis' and encouraging my students to consider the wider history surrounding the various composers' lives and the philosophical influences these had on their creativity. As well, I had a busy private piano practice. It was indeed very full-on. It was not always easy...some financial stress at times. Always managed. My husband working so hard. Both of us working so hard. A lot of family coming and going. Celebrations, great family dinners with much discussion and argument, some serious 'talking to's when needed, teenage broken hearts quickly mended, a crisis here and there; but generally, it all worked. It was a reassuringly solid family situation. Overall, Life was good.

While still a member of the VMTA, I hit upon the idea of offering small winter gatherings of music teachers in our home, for discussions about and performances of Music. These casual gatherings around a large open fire, were called "**The Fireside Music Society** "and were happy casual occasions.Following suggestions, the **Fireside Music Society** became a series of private concerts. I enjoyed so much this sharing...

sharing of something special which can bring so much joy to many, and mixing with the fine artists who performed for us.

Every winter, for seven, perhaps eight years, we offered private concerts in our home, about five monthly ones each year. The standard of the artists performing at these events was extremely high. We had many leading Australian musicians (pianists, string and wind players, and chamber groups) as well as visiting artists from abroad who were already involved in an Australian tour. Included were several from the Martin Piano Trio, two recitals from one of Australia's leading concert pianists, Ronald Farren-Price, who had performed so often around the world, the Acacia Quartet, The Team of Pianists, London-based Ruth Nye, (who was on a performing tour of Australia), Michael Brimer, international 'cellist, Richard Markson, with whom I remember playing the beautiful Fauré Elegie, Op.24, and many more. Mack Jost visited, Di Bresciani, Piers Lane, so many fine artists gathering on those winter evenings in our home for music, wine and conversation. It was wonderful.

Now, in describing a private home with room enough for quite large audiences listening to excellent artists might conjure up a beautiful salon in a very large house. No, in this case, far from it. It was a home of just average size…charm yes, but not huge. We did have a fairly large l-shaped sitting room opening on to a terrace and with a large fireplace. There was a study opening off it, and there was the grand piano etc. But the setting up for these concerts is a story in itself. They would never have been possible in that particular room without the dedicated assistance of a young Chilean friend, Jim Pena. Jim was one of those remarkable young men who can turn their hands to anything. Fleeing the Pinochet regime with his parents and several brothers and sisters, the family had settled in Melbourne. Jim's education had been interrupted so he had arrived with no formal qualifications. Determined to succeed, he started out doing gardening jobs, (which is how we discovered him) and gradually we realised Jim was a very competent carpenter, could fix anything including electrical gadgets. But more importantly, he often presented wide ranging ideas for discussion which were well considered intelligent ones, as he carefully but surely conquered the language. Gradually, Jim became part of our family. His stories of life under the Pinochet regime and fleeing Chile were fascinating for Justin, our twelve-year-old youngest. We also soon realised that Jim appreciated music, art and the finer things of life and was very happy indeed to become the principal "mover and shaker" for facilitating these new concerts.

Of course the open fires had to go and the piano was moved by him each time down to the corner of that l-shaped room, beside the fireplace just before the tuner arrived. Then much of the furniture was manouvred by Jim to upstairs bedrooms or the basement, after which he would collect and arrange the hired folding chairs sometimes for about forty people. An incredible effort each time. Without Jim and his enthusiasm it could never have happened. After all this physical effort, on the evenings of the concerts, he would don crisp white shirt and black bow tie and be there to assist in any way, including serving après-concert champers and chicken sandwiches I had made that afternoon. Jim always listened very carefully to the music and I recall his delight when on different occasions, both Ruth Nye and her brother, Ronald Farren-Price, performed for us. He had known that both had studied with the great Chilean maestro, Claudio Arrau (who had refused ever to return to Santiago till Pinochet was finished). How he knew this I never knew, perhaps from the written program notes I prepared for each concert. But he was very excited to be able to speak about Arrau with them both. Jim today has gone on to raise a successful family with tertiary qualifications and runs his own very successful business. We are so proud of our Jim.

The five concerts each winter became very successful events. After each, the male guests helped by stacking the chairs to one side, Jim and I (and whoever else in the family happened to be around) then served the drinks and sandwiches I had made that afternoon. Conversations were lively and interesting among our sometimes quite distinguished guests. Dear friends, Judy and Gordon Cope-Williams, came down from their Romsey vineyard and enjoyed some concerts so much that LINGUA MUSICA later assisted in setting up Judy's wonderful and continuing Sunday concerts. Near neighbour, Shirley Nicholas, usually brought her friend, Lady Viola Tait. One evening after a concert, the happy party went on later than usual, so our son, Gavin, tried to persuade Shirley to leave her car and allow him to drive them home. "I'll bring it round to your place tomorrow" he said. Shirley insisted she was fine. Alas, on the way to Viola's, they had an accident and were taken to hospital. I was not informed till the next morning. We were so shocked. But thank heavens neither was hurt and soon permitted to return to their homes. Shirley Nicholas was a great patron of the Arts in Melbourne (including the Hephzibah Menuhin Scholarship), as well as having an abiding interest in and support of a handicapped childrens' research foundation. She was a very special person, great fun to be with, and we attended several concerts and other outings together. Shirley was the widow of George Nicholas, the founder of Nicholas Aspro. Interestingly, George's two children, Nola and Lindsay Nicholas, respectively, had married the famous violinist, Yehudi Menuhin, and his equally talented sister, Hephzibah. That episode was an amazing story in itself...enough for several books, which of course have indeed been written by several eminent writers. Most of those books are actually about Yehudi and the Menuhin Family. Hephzibah was always included as also was their sister, Yaltah, but it was not till Australian author, Jacqueline Kent, wrote her marvellous "An Exacting Heart" that a work had actually been totally dedicated to the extraordinary life of Hephzibah Menuhin (Nicholas) and her attempts to settle down in country Victoria. She did so much work from their property, "Terrinalum" near Mortlake in Western Victoria to organise a travelling library and so much more for the education of local children. She was not only a great pianist but an extraordinary human being.

Later on (when LINGUA MUSICA was an on-going reality), Viola Tait was anxious for me to visit the chateau of her daughter, Isla, in the South of France, with a view to including it on a music tour. I did visit and had a delightful short time with Isla and her husband. We wandered around discussing possible locations in the grounds for a performance. But though a very charming small chateau in pretty gardens, regretfully it was isolated and would have presented too many practical problems for a group visit.

Before each concert commenced, our youngest son, Justin, enjoyed sitting at a small table in the porch, ticking off the names on the booking sheet and collecting any fees owing.(It was obvious even at fourteen, he was showing signs of later business acumen!) I had estimated prices so as to be able to pay the correct professional fees to our performers... everything else was provided by us plus always the gifted bottles of champagne from various local supporters. The concerts used to be advertised in the 'local rag ', and bookings were essential. I do recall though on one occasion there were a couple of young women enjoying their drinks but who looked a little lost. I managed to speak with them and discovered they were music students and had sneaked in via the basement. Despite initial embarrassment about being 'sprung', they were quite open about it, and though a bit concerned about the obvious lack of security on that occasion, I found them to be delightful and was very glad they had been able to enjoy the performances they had obviously travelled quite a distance to hear. (A mental note was made that we needed to make certain in future that that bottom door was securely locked.)

On several occasions we had piano concerto performances, which of course required a second piano and pianist to play the orchestral reductions, and the necessary tuning. On almost all occasions, a neighbour's borrowed upright was brought in, but I remember that once, a second 'grand' was offered by one of the performers and accepted....well, not one of my best decisions, I have to say. The room as a result was so overcrowded, several guests had to listen from the adjacent study. It worked... just. But a situation better not repeated.

I do remember that on two occasions during those years, I myself played the beautiful **Mozart Concerto No 23, in A major, K.488** on my own piano, with different associated artists playing the orchestral reductions on the other. And I also did some solos and took part in some chamber music presentations (the wonderful **G minor Piano Quartet of Mozart** with three members of a very good quartet springs to mind); and my daughter, Jacqueline, once performed the **Bach A minor violin concerto** with me. But there were many others I needed to practise pretty hard for as well as all the accompanying of various instrumentalists. It was challenging, and very good for me, demanding I find time in my busy schedule for some much needed regular practice, and kept me up to scratch!

It was after one of these winter concerts, perhaps during winter 1987, that one of the guests, highly involved in the travel industry, suggested to me that I do a LINGUA MUSICA European music tour. I was very amused. Me? I? Running a tour? (Visions of a harassed woman striding ahead of a large group holding up a furled umbrella, such as I had seen on my travels, sprang to mind. What a ghastly thought!) And the suggestion was laughingly dismissed. I was a professional musician, heavens above! He raised it again at a concert the following year. I still considered the idea to be totally beyond consideration. But my architect son, Brendan, persuaded me at least to give it some thought. "You know a lot about Music. You know quite a lot about Europe. Don't simply dismiss the idea. Give it some thought." My husband agreed. "Give it some thought."

It took several months of "giving it some thought" and continuing to reject the idea as being absurd, before I slowly began to come round. I began (just began, mind you) to think about what would be involved in order to create from scratch such a tour. I knew absolutely nothing about organising any such thing. However, little by little, the ideas took hold, my enthusiasm grew and I actually began to feel it just might be possible to have such an adventure! Over the coming summer holidays, free from teaching, and in between family holiday commitments, I pored over all the various articles I could lay my hands on (no Google in those days) and began to realise that though there were many organised European tours from Australia in various areas, I could see little evidence of there being many (if any) in the field of Music.

How different it was then, when my new Music Tours were the only ones advertised, to several years later, when the success of LINGUA MUSICA seemed to encourage one after another competitive such tour. I even remember reading exactly my own words being used in some printed presentations till I realised one needed to put a copyright on them. Even then it didn't stop. I amusingly recall **Margaret Whitlam**, for example, when we first met at a Bermagui Festival, laughing when she heard my name. "Oh Roma Randles! I have been collecting your brochures for years! Love your tour outlines. Am going to do a Mozart one". We enjoyed a lively and happy conversation about European tours in general. I confess to feeling more flattered than annoyed because of the approval of such a distinguished person as Margaret Whitlam, considered a 'National Treasure'. And then I later discovered she produced a tour the following year entitled "Mostly Mozart ", so much of it based on my own! Oh well...... In her later book, "My Other World", Margaret spoke about wonderful travel with husband Gough,(walking encyclopaedia that he was), of her absolute delight in learning about new cultures and making it possible for others to do the same. She created and ran herself extremely successful educative tours on a variety of topics, in an enormous variety of locations. Her ability, charm and enormous wit, come through so readily in this captivating account. She came to a decision to run a Music one quite late, and am not sure how this would have gone, because of course, Margaret Whitlam, though so often to be seen at concerts with her husband, (so different from our present lot!) was certainly no musician herself. BUT, as she had said, she had been collecting my brochures for years! Sadly, just as she was about to leave on this tour, she tripped and injured her hip, so that was the end of that. After reading it, I became even more protective of my ankles! So easily done and can put a full stop to all plans in less than a minute!

Anyway, to cut a long story short, by mid-January 1988 I had become engaged in creating that first tour...really, an Investigative kind of tour, with several friends from our London days joining me. I needed to learn the ropes, and when there were any problems, my friends would laughingly say, "Well you fix it...you're the Tour Leader!" We visited Glyndebourne, Aldeburgh, Paris, Avignon, Bordeaux and back to London.We had a lot of fun. I made masses of notes. And UTA French Airlines paid my expenses. I felt reasonably encouraged to put together and offer a PROPER tour for the following year, **"Aldeburgh and Beyond ".** Back home, my busy life continued, but later in that year, working whenever I could, setting up advertisements in the press, and lo and behold, by mid-February 1989, had begun to accept bookings. Actual bookings! My first brochures were created(methods as described previously) and by the end of May we were off and running. *LINGUA MUSICA EUROPEAN MUSIC TOURS* was truly an established entity and continuing!

"ALDEBURGH AND BEYOND"

1989: Well, there I was, flying off to London and elsewhere for the necessary pre-tour double-checking of everything I had put in place. This first "proper" tour attempt was a fairly unusual one…intentionally so. In this way I thought it had had more chance of grabbing attention. This was the first…the first…and I was anxious, excited, terrified, confident, anxious, in quick succession. It just HAD to go well..but would it? Yes nervous indeed…a glass of bubbly here and there on flight helped…well, a bit.

The Itinerary I had put together: London (Sightseeing, opera, a great gallery, food, concerts); **The Bath Festival :The Aldeburgh International Festival: Paris** (similar arrangements as in London; **Chartres** (a visit with expert to the great Chartres Cathedral and its spectacular stained glass windows); **Bordeaux** (with as its highlight, a piano recital by Claudio Arrau in the Grand Théâtre); Chateauroux (and time to spend at nearby **Nohant** and the home of Chopin and George Sand, and other medieval villages in the region); back to **Paris** for a final Performance and Farewell Dinner. Not bad for a first off? (Glyndebourne had to be dismissed that year…it happened later in the summer.)

The first couple of days were spent staying with dear friends in Kent who drove me around as I checked London hotel, concert venues, guides, chosen restaurants, etc. Then I rented a car and drove down to **BATH** in Somerset, then back north/east to **SUFFOLK**…all this at rather breakneck speed, and was followed by a quick flight across to **PARIS** for everything necessary there, a train to **CHARTRES,** where I had a couple of meetings, and on to **BORDEAUX** and collecting tickets and other arrangements in that complicated city and its wineries. Whew! Another rented car had me driving north/east to the River Indre region (and Chopin's country home at **NOHANT**), a solitary drive I recall I adored, having not been in this region for several years. A final train hop back to Paris...and another quick hop back to London. Whew again! This had all been accomplished in five very concentrated days and I was already badly in need of a holiday. But no. One day off for a bit of rest, the hairdresser, a shoe repair, and then the next, a 5pm Reception and dinner for my group. From then on I was conducting my first LINGUA MUSICA tour! I could scarcely believe it! I was as excited as everyone else appeared to be...and they were a very nice, compatible middle-aged, music-loving group of nine, three married couples and the rest singles. I just knew we were all going to have a fantastic time. And we did. Never mind the few little hiccups along the way....losing Joan for two hours in Bath, Lisa needing urgent dental treatment in London just before our flight to Paris, Paul turning his ankle in Chartres and unable to walk.... and absolutely beyond belief, arriving at our hotel in Bordeaux to find that Claudio Arrau had just that day, cancelled his recital because of illness, (the first of several such cancellations the maestro was forced to make as his strength began to fail.) But we survived it all...the answer, as always, to be able to produce a sound Plan B, and to have the full understanding and support of one's group.

THE BATH FESTIVAL:

The beautiful UNESCO-listed Georgian city of Bath, Somerset, has been attracting English and international visitors for many years. Its particular lay-out, the hot springs of its Roman Baths, the elegant Palladian architecture of Royal Crescent, its literature and music, are of the highest order. Looking right back, in 1668, Elizabeth 1st came to Bath particularly to hear the Wells Cathedral Choir sing in Bath Abbey. The city has very many beautiful venues which have been used for its Music Festival founded in 1948 and continuing till 2017. Yehudi Menuhin acted as Artistic Director from 1959-1968, and so many distinguished classical musicians have performed for packed audiences over two weeks late Spring/early Summer each year. Over time, Jazz, Folk and World Music have been additions, as well as Literature and a Festival for Children. There is also of course a well run Jane Austen tour (she was a resident of Bath at one time), and many other interesting attractions. It is not only a culturally rich city but now also a very modern one, with an amazing number of pubs, cafes and restaurants.

After four busy days in London, our group enjoyed a well planned 3 days in Bath, including two beautiful performances. I remember so well the recital by the great Austrian pianist, Alfred Brendel, and his habit of sometimes staring up at the ceiling in contemplation as he played. What a great master this artist is, musician, writer, poet, increasing arthritis forcing him to give his last public performance in Vienna in 2008…he, who once famously remarked, "I am by nature a pessimist who always enjoys being pleasantly surprised "! We stayed on this occasion at the charming Royal Crescent Hotel.

Our good natured and knowledgeable driver made our full day trip in our private minivan through beautiful and highly varied countryside from Somerset in the West to Suffolk on the East Coast, a most delightful experience, and with interesting stops along the way.

THE ALDEBURGH INTERNATIONAL FESTIVAL :

ALDEBURGH close to the Suffolk Coast, is about 160 kms east of London. The renowned British composer, **BENJAMIN BRITTEN (1913-1976)**, had grown up in this quiet, peaceful corner of England, with its restful landscape, small villages and interesting little coastal towns with pebbly beaches overlooking the North Sea. The coastline is dotted with quaint pubs, cottages and fishermen's shacks, (albeit not the kind of beaches to which we Australians are drawn), which became very popular as hide-away sojourns, and soon enough as a drawcard for the wonderful music festival created by Benjamim Britten and his professional and personal partner of forty years, the wonderful English tenor, **PETER PEARS.** Living and working together in THE RED HOUSE on the outskirts of the village of **Snape**, on the edge of the meandering River Alde, they of course were careful about the existing social and legal mores of the time, having separate bedrooms (!) and for maintaining the necessary individual concentration for their work, using separate studios...one a purpose built one beside the charming house. Their physical fitness was maintained by playing tennis. Britten wrote so many large works, his wonderful Violin Concerto I adore, and operas like 'Peter Grimes' in his twentieth century style of composition. For me, his most superb opus is his great WAR REQUIEM...which I ensured my group would know about by given a lecture on it and playing for them a recording of this dramatic and intensely moving composition, composed by Britten for the sanctification of the new Coventry Cathedral, which had been destroyed in a WW2 bombing raid, (sad ramifications later with the bombing of Dresden.)

Snape Maltings is the name given to the Arts Complex created from the old Maltings on the estuary of the river, where historically, barley was malted as part of the beer making process. Snape itself had been an energised industrialised centre for about 175 years. Still a thriving commercial little place, full of interesting art, craft and book shops and great food centres. The little pub, "The Plough and Sail "is a cheerful and popular one in which to while away an hour or three. The Aldeburgh Festival had its beginning in 1948, and has become one of the truly important ones on the world classical music scene. Over the years, so many distinguished international musicians have taken part, Yehudi Menuhin and the great cellist, Rostropovitch, being only two such. The Jubilee Hall, churches and other venues continue to be used, but the principal one is of course the remarkable **Snape Maltings.**

Our group, whilst staying for four nights in an old inn overlooking the sea, enjoyed everything this region had to offer, including two lovely concerts. In early June that year I recall The London Sinfionetta, conducted by Oliver Knussen, and Steven Isserlis, Cello, playing with the

Scottish Chamber Orchestra. Their program consisted of **Mendelssohn: Overture to a "Midsummer Night's Dream"**, Britten: **Symphony for Orchestra and Cello, Op 68,** Maxwell Davis: **"An Old Orkney Wedding ",** Beethoven: **Symphony No 8** (so perfect in such an idyllic pastoral setting) and much more. There were also interesting interviews and talks. In Snape Maltings as always on later tours, I included free time for rest and individual walks, discovery and reflection. This free time is an absolutely necessary component of any successful tour. Rest and a break from the 'togetherness' are needed. And it is not a good idea just to attend a concert...one needs time to absorb and reflect on the experience. Most on that tour were not used to such considerations, but once we discussed the relevance of such reflection, they quickly realised how beneficial it was to do so.

I like to discuss the actual form of the works my travellers hear and the historic influences, and as well, to ponder the ephemeral nature of SOUND, its phenomenology, and how Sound engages the mind, soul and body...a topic which fascinates me.

A very happy group was driven from Aldeburgh to Heathrow for our flight to Paris, the next leg of this unusual tour.

PARIS: Well, what can I say about Paris, which hasn't been said a thousand times better than I before? People "know" Paris, even if they have never been there. The City of Light, arguably the most beautiful in the world, was the next stop on that magical first tour. Staying in a charming hotel in my favourite part of Paris, the Left Bank, we enjoyed as much as possible all the Latin Quarter offered. I had organised it all ahead...the guides who gave the history, the organised sightseeing of all the famous monuments, including the Eiffel Tower with its unfortunate queues, a half day of gallery visiting with an art expert, (so full that it permitted me time to sneak off alone to my favourite, the wonderful Musée Rodin), a bateau mouche cruise, one opera at the gorgeous old Opera Garnier, and an excellent concert at the Salle Pleyel. A little time to shop in the Galleries Lafayette, time for personal discoveries, some great food and wines...and soon we were headed for the Gare de Montparnasse for our TGV fast train to **CHARTRES,** not much more than an hour away. Those TGV's were such fascinating experiences for my groups....trains of Grande Vitesse, sitting in their first class seats with the French countryside whizzing past their large windows at enormous speed. CHARTRES is a beautiful city, S/W of Paris, and most noted for its wonderful cathedral with its inspiring stained glass windows. I had arranged on my previous quick trip for a lecture and tour of the cathedral to be given by a distinguished medieval architect who was living there at the time and making an in-depth study of this great edifice for his coming book. I think this was a great coup...he was not a tour guide! It is a unique and awe-inspiring medieval structure and as I had been there so recently, and also with my family some years back, I took the opportunity to head off for a solitary walk and a welcome coffee and reading the paper on the heavily timbered deck of a charming local cafe. A little time alone every now and then, silence, mental recovery, right from the beginning, was always important.

After lunch we continued by fast train to Bordeaux, changing at Tours, which was quite easy. It was a pleasant and relaxing four hour journey, arriving into Bordeaux Gare St.Jean late afternoon. As usual it took a little time to get everyone's passports and room keys and luggage organised and have them assisted to their rooms. Finally arriving in my own, I found a note on the table... *"Madame Randles, nous avons le regret de vous announcer que le concert offert par le Maestro, Claudio Arrau, grand théâtre a dû être annulé. Nous vous prions de vous metre eu contact avec le Bureau de Reservations demain"*.

Shock horror! This was the reason for coming to Bordeaux! I rang the Bureau...naturally closed. But a message announced this cancellation due to the sudden ill health of Maestro Claudio Arrau and that refunds could be collected. Over the planned dinner that evening in a restaurant along the River Garonne, I broke the news. They had already been given so much information about this famous pianist and the program he would perform. All were disappointed of course, but perhaps none so much as I. During their sight-seeing tour with our guide next morning, I searched and discovered another concert (which seemed likely to be a nice Piano Trio one) in a beautiful church nearby, bought tickets for that and joined the long queue for refunds at the Booking Office in the Grand Théatre. A river trip, an afternoon visiting two great vineyards after a delicious lunch at the first, more discovery of this beautiful but quite complicated city and its bridges and our three days otherwise passed happily.

9am, next morning, and Jacques, our French driver ("Call me Jack ") arrived in hotel reception, panting and apologetic about being a little late. "The breedge traffic unbelievable!" With the help of a porter he quickly had the luggage plus us on board his very smart and roomy red minibus and with some soothing Mozart playing on the intercom, negotiated the said indeed heavy traffic, and before too long, we were over the river and cruising along towards the beautiful region of the Dordogne. Several stops en route for short tours, coffees, lunch etc in Bergerac, Perigeux, Sarlat and other delightful and much loved places of this region, which the English had already begun to think of as their own, much to the annoyance of the locals. A really beautiful drive, with many contrasts and with informed and often amusing commentaries from Jacques so that early evening found us driving into the sweeping grounds of our Chateauroux hotel and looking forward to a much later summer dinner on the terrace overlooking its extensive gardens and swimming pool.

There was Jacques (call me Jack) again next morning, full of enthusiasm, to take us not very far in this pretty region of the River Indre, to LA CHÂTRE, and very close by, NOHANT, with its **Chateau de Nohant** (actually more of a country manor house than a chateau), where Frédéric Chopin had lived for several years with his lover, George Sand, on her family estate.(This was the pseudonym for the most famous French novelist of the time, Amatine Lucile Aurore Dupin, known to all as Aurore).Chopin, the extreme master of the piano during this Romantic Age, was not strong in health. In many ways, Aurore, several years older than Frederic over-mothered and criticised him and this caused much friction. Nonetheless the two worked extremely well on their respective professional pursuits there at Nohant. But the weekends were left free to welcome visits from Parisian friends like Franz Liszt and other notables. The brilliant Liszt was always very complimentary about Chopin's compositions. (We actually don't read anything about the reverse which is strange…or not?) It is not hard to imagine riotous weekends of music, conversation, great food and wine, riding in the surrounding woods, discussions and sometimes fierce arguments about the current artistic and political developments in the capital. Current Politics was a very strong subject. Perhaps it always is among the cognoscenti? The house today has been left exactly as it was, even to the placement of the furniture, so my group very much enjoyed the time spent with a guide, roaming through the beautiful rooms and gardens before late lunch at a picturesque inn in nearby La Châtre, followed by a well-considered Chopin piano recital. Next day we visited several delightful medieval villages in the region and walked by the lovely river with its banks of willows gently moving in the breeze. A swim in our hotel's large pool for some and another relaxed dinner on the terrace brought a very interesting and happy day to an end. This dinner was in fact our Farewell one and I recall many toasts and much happy reminiscing about our wonderful experiences. An unexpected and delightful surprise was the gift they had bought for me in Bordeaux (a charming gesture, almost always repeated at the conclusion of other tours).

PARIS: After a lazy morning in the grounds, early next afternoon, we took another great TGV 2 hour trip from Chateauroux back to Paris and our Latin Quarter hotel. We dressed up for our final musical experience….opera at the very modern Paris Opera Bastille. What a magnificent modern structure, but oh so different from the Garnier. Afterwards we wandered along the fascinating streets of the Quartier Marais, with plans for us to meet for a champagne breakfast next morning, before I accompanied them to Charles de Gaulle Airport. Most were returning to Australia or London, one couple opting to continue their travels elsewhere.

I remember waving them off with a combined sense of sadness, satisfaction and relief. It had worked! Everyone was happy! I was happy. I was also exhausted! The strain of all that organisation, all that responsibility, the constant talking, the fixing up on occasions when things had not gone absolutely according to plan, were truly exhausting. I really had had no idea. In no way had I been prepared for how full on it would be!

An airport cafe with comfortable looking lounge seats looked a good idea. I sank into one and ordered a light lunch, with a glass of Sancerre, plus un cafe.

Later, somewhat revived, I collected the pre-booked small car (a little Renault I think) and drove out of the airport surrounds, negotiated the Périférique, and on to the N4 heading N/W to the tiny seaside town of Etrétat, where I had promised myself a two day recovery sojourn. That evening, hunched over the tiny desk in my equally tiny room overlooking the sea, I sought to bring all the accounting up to date. All through the tour I had kept regular nightly accounting in my log book. Major fixtures had been paid well before departure, but there are always additional costs as the tours progressed. I anxiously totalled them. I checked and double checked together with all the major pre-paid costs. I could hardly believe it. Far from running into debt, I had made a small profit of $940!! (Business people would laugh at the smallness of this of course, especially after such a tour...but I had not lost!). I could now relax. And began to wonder what on earth professional tour companies did with their much much higher tour prices. A beautiful day wandering Etretat and its famous cliffs next morning was anticipated and probably a few 'dropping- off' moments as well. My first LINGUA MUSICA TOUR! I went down to the outdoor bar, looking forward to a celebratory glass, even if on my own.

It actually took me three days to get myself back to Paris, as I wandered along the coast, rediscovering gorgeous Honfleur, which, as a family, we had always loved, and now made a mental note to include on some future tour...there is an excellent Erik Satie Museum here. Trouville / Deauville (even taking in an unexpected beautiful lunchtime organ concert in the cathedral), and eastwards back to the great city, stopping off at Monet's lovely house and Garden in Giverny. It was so enjoyable and relaxing and as well, really useful research for some point in the future.I continuously scribbled many notes with exact contact details, distances etc.

UTA French Airlines had given me another free long distance return flight and some accommodation, but internal flights and train trips were expensive, so had better do my research for any further tour the following year right now. This I did. And also, looking ahead a little, I knew 1991 would be the greatly anticipated "Mozart Bicentenial". Flushed with the success of my first one, I thought I might just put together an offer for this European Mozart celebration that year as well as the next. At this stage, so far ahead and only a 'maybe' but advance research certainly worthwhile. But this had to be pretty jolly quick. Off I went, by plane, train and rent-a-car on an exhausting gallop to investigate possibilities. I remember at Salzburg Hofbahnhof, asking for directions to the Mozart Bicentenial Office and was amazed to find it was an actual a large building containing **many** Mozart offices and large staff already planning 1991 in that city. Obviously going to be BIG! My charming and very glamorous consultant was absolutely intrigued to discover I was all the way from Australia, and planning a possible group tour. Grüss Gott! On the plane back to Australia, I remember doodling many little route possibilities....before falling into the deepest of deep sleeps.

CELEBRATING MOZART TOUR

Back home my busy life continued....family, teaching, the concerts, school involvements (my own and those of my children). But when time permitted, I shut myself away down in the basement and worked on my tours, the next one and a further one...a Mozart tour for 1991. First establish a definite route and then the inclusions, which of course required not only my own plans, but assurances from the European organisers of definite performances on definite dates. (For later tours, this was always the main problem, because performance details are rarely available as early as one would wish; but for this huge Mozart Year Celebration, all were fixed two years ahead, which certainly simplified matters for me on the other side of the world.)

UTA FRENCH AIRLINES were extremely supportive and advised that a good registered agent would be a valuable assett. In fact, the Law demands that making airline bookings on behalf of others can only be done through a registered agent. From now on I wished to offer the entire package....including flights. They recommended a colleague, whose office was in Collins Street, and Roy Manning was indeed a great help and became a good friend. He was, I think, rather intrigued to find himself dealing with, not a travel agent, but this lone female musician, with a large family, doing what I had done and was now proposing to continue. Once I had put the1991 itinerary together and had advertised it in the Press, my colourful brochures, ("cutting and pasting" Roma -style) were soon ready and the enquiries flooded in. I had advised all to be directed to my new registered agent, who processed them and passed the finished ones on to me. Roy also dealt with the money. Enquiries of course do not mean Bookings. Many people were just curious, some total time-wasters, and also the "If only"s, with whom I would have lovely warm conversations. I recall one extraordinarily interested woman who was obviously making very exact notes. She did this on several different calls. Then she said blithely, "All this sounds just great…my husband and I will use these routes and hotels when we go ourselves later this year!" I did feel really furious with myself for being taken in so easily by this shameless approach….but heave ho…nothing to be done about it. A very useful learning experience. Just don't be so open and informative in future till a deposit is paid. Booking forms containing the Tour Conditions which had to be accepted and signed, and deposit and final payment details were sent out with directions that the completed forms and cheques be sent to Collins St. It was not very long before Roy rang me: "There are already twenty official bookings. How much longer do you wish to continue?" It was all pretty amazing, and to be fitted into an already busy family life. I seem to remember that I let Roy go to 25 bookings.

So now the setting up and securely putting in place every single component of this tour began in earnest. I had to make absolutely sure everything promised in that colourful brochure would indeed happen! This is the most time consuming and stressful part of any tour structuring. And I was not part of any company…I was a 'one man band'! I had to do it all. I was down in that basement very late at night. The fax machine ran hot, even at ridiculous hours after arriving home from some function, every evening and very early mornings. Group booking prices are usually less than individual prices. My policy was always to reject even this lower group offer as being "beyond the budget of this tour".

It still amazes me how immediately this tactic brought the response of an even lower group offer, which I would accept. Thankfully in those early days, accommodation deposits were not demanded immediately… there would be a set date ahead, and cancellation policies were manageable. This easy situation changed entirely before many years passed.

However, tickets for the performances were quite another matter and the incoming deposits were rarely enough to cover this so I often had to 'go out on a limb' to secure tickets for our group, hoping that the balance of their fees would eventually cover it. They always did. The Salzburg Festival tickets were the most expensive of all (and have continued to be so....absolutely outrageous now.) Once I had to borrow for two months so I could safely secure those Salzburg tickets before they ran out the door. Of course there were all the other components to secure...means of travel, drivers, guides, art experts, meals (all those menus! Always a challenge... making sure Jewish and other dietary requirements were catered for), wonderful excursions from each location, lectures, and my new idea... the writing and colourfully illustrating of what I now called the **TOUR HANDBOOK,** (copied for every participant), which contained a daily schedule, information about every location, every artist and ensemble, history, occasional articles/essays, and an analysis of every musical work to be encountered. (My beloved 'Form and Analysis' interest and knowledge coming to the fore here).This latter I considered to be my "learning whilst travelling" effort for my participants. I did really wish that my tours were also educative ones..."Learning Whilst Travelling "I advised my participants. I know of no other tours which offer such detailed Handbooks like this. It was quite an effort and always most appreciated; and many people tell me they have kept them and still enjoy referring to them every now and then.

So finally it was all in place, and now there was set up a wonderful LINGUA MUSICA celebration of Mozart in **PARIS, VIENNA, SALZBURG, INNSBRUCK, LUZERN,** a three day holiday break in gorgeous **INTERLAKEN,** and continuing in **MONTREUX, GENEVA** and finishing in **NICE**, where there was a large international airport, so that everyone could either return to Paris for their homeward long haul flight, or continue their travels with ease. Yes, it was a rather long tour...I hoped not TOO long, and that the three day break in the middle was a perfect solution. There was another reason I had included Nice. So often thought of as just a tourist spot, it is anything **but**! A University city, the fourth largest in France, it has major art galleries, a wonderful Conservatoire, several concert halls and even an Opera House and so much more of cultural value. It has also the richness and beauty of its location on the Mediterranean and easy access to all the smaller and artistically important places nearby. There was also another much more personal reason to include it, having been a very favourite location for years for our young family when we lived in England...not in Nice proper, but up in the hills above....our caravanning days, which I recall with such delight. (Of course this personal info was not revealed in the printed tour materials!

"**AND THEN GOD CREATED MOZART!** "I remember reading this statement by some writer in the Guardian all those years ago, and also E.T.A. Hoffmann's observations about Mozart's music being "....the mysterious language of a distant spiritual kingdom".

Musicologist, Nicholas Till, said that "Mozart was working at just that moment in Western history when Art was assuming its modern role as a secular substitute for religion. And Music, during the 18th century, was the most spiritual of the arts...the pure art." Oh, such inspired writing! Such veritas. All noble thoughts, and yes, I probably agreed with them, even if rather beyond my own powers of literary expression. But the tour I was constructing was actually celebrating a brilliant life that ended with a far too early death in December 1791. I would just do it my own way, as best I could.

Wolfgang Amadeus Mozart (1756 – 1791) born in Salzburg and died in Vienna. Most of the popular details of his life and the tragedy of his early death would be known to all those who were anxious to come on this Mozart tour. But naturally, they would find a lot more detailed information about our hero in their new Tour Handbook, not forgetting the various lectures. His life (worryingly poor, rich, colourful, brilliant, desperate, joyful, sad) and his Masonic connections are usually well known. His inspiration and intuition had arrived effortlessly from a certain realm. His compositions included marvellous concertos, piano sonatas, sonatas for piano with other instruments, great symphonies, chamber music of great renown, string quartets, and oh, so much more, including Opera...especially Opera. Who was it who once wrote, "In every work Mozart composed, there is a glimpse of an opera trying to get out "? I often think of this when playing (or teaching) Mozart. Yes, one needs some delicacy, a little restraint...but I personally love what I call "his g minor moments"...not necessarily in that key either! An extraordinary, tragically short life of an extraordinary man. So much obviously known already. So much extra through further personal research. But how to use it all to create a very special tour? Salzburg perhaps? Salzburg has always claimed Mozart, but in actual fact, he hated the place and couldn't get away quickly enough from the detested Archbishop who ruled his life there, in order to pursue an independent career in Vienna.

Over-the-top European celebrations were planned for the entire year, 1991. My research led me to believe that a tour built before and after the famous Salzburg Festival would work and this is what I put in place. A meeting at Ch de Gaulle, Paris on August 22nd and farewelling from the Aeroport de Nice on September 16th...a very full tour with enormous variety of content (both musical **and** otherwise) in a wealth of fabulous locations. Maybe it was a little too long? Yes, it probably was. To counteract this, I planned a three day "holiday break" in the middle of our itinerary. This is what I offered and people seemed to absolutely love the entire idea, including the mid-tour break.

SOME HIGHLIGHTS 1991 :

PARIS: Mozart actually disliked Paris, but it was here that UNESCO organised an enormous programme in the Sorbonne to mark his death in December 1791; and it was here that we attended an Opera Garnier gala of **"The Marriage of Figaro "**, a well remembered Mozart piano recital at Radio France, an address by a distinguished international musicologist, a beautiful Bach Double Concerto in the historic Eglise St Germain des Pres, and much more. A comfortable Air France flight brought us to **VIENNA** (the city Mozart had adopted and where he spent most of his composing life). Such an atmosphere! "Grüss Gott"! It was an extravagant abundance of musical wealth here: visiting Mozart's house (known as 'The Figaro House'!), the great St Stephen's cathedral, his own parish church, St Michael's, where we were ushered to the very front pews and actually took an active part, assisting at a commemorative Mass, one of our group requested to help give out the Communion (such a brief but well remembered time for spiritual reflection.) Wonderful restaurants and cafes (including famous DEMEL and Clive's marvellous address, the famous Vienna Opera Haus, concerts in different venues, including the wonderful Musikverein, and our stay in the delightful boutique Hotel Wandl (which I have continued to use every time I visit Vienna). I even included a visit to the most famous music shop, "Doplinger" in the Dorotheegasse. (I still have the old score of a Beethoven String Quartet I bought there.) So so much more in Vienna and also the beautiful excursions. One in particular, we all loved and actually one I personally had never done before...a trip down the Danube to MELK and its magnificent Benedictine Abbey, the oldest in Europe, with its incredible glinting gold leaf ceiling (which had never been retouched), and enormous library full of treasures where students from all over the world come to study Latin. (Reading some of the magnificent scrolls, I tried to remember sufficient Latin from my two years of Latin at school. Well, I tried. I did manage a little!) This Abbey, one time host to Maria Theresa and Joseph 11, also suffered an uninvited guest...Napoleon arriving (with 20,000 men stationed nearby!)

This was such a leisurely and delightful river trip. We enjoyed conversations as we sailed along and got to know one another a little better. Some amusing stories: One guest, Peter, had lost his front crown that morning, so resourceful fellow as he was, he went out and bought some glue. "Will do till I can get to a dentist" he said. And this leads to the discovery that they were old friends of very dear dental friends of ours in Melbourne, the Wardlaws. Another guest, Lois, we found, knew well the Spanish restaurant at the Brisbane Expo which my then undergraduate architect son had been sent to design several years before (quite an honour for this young final year student). And another, astute Louise from Melbourne, had read in the Age a couple of letters our youngest, Justin, had contributed. She quoted them almost word for word. (Lord knows now what that was all about!) But this is what happens on a leisurely L/M cruise...we get to know one another.

A lovely train trip took us on to **SALZBURG** and our very lively guide, Gudula, always in national dress of colourful dirndl and apron with white full sleeved blouse, took over. Here the music performances I had reserved were wonderful and included an experience of the great Mozart Requiem in Salzburg Cathedral, given by the Vienna Philharmonic Orchestra and conducted by Carl Maria Guillini. Unforgettable! Our European Travel consultants, CITYRAMA, with whom I had collaborated, had so far done us proud in Paris, and Vienna...always the best buses, always the most elegantly served meals, and the best guides. Now here in Salzburg, their Gudula was a great hit! She showed off Salzburg to its very best advantage, also its fabulous mountain and lakes surrounds, "The Salzgammergut "one of the most glorious regions I know. We visited the little churchyard of St Peter's, where Wolfgang and his sister, Nannerl, are buried, we had fabulous meals (one on top of the amazing Hohensalzburg Fortress with an equally amazing sunset), and of course our several further very important music performances...the most significant of these being best seats in the Festival Haus for Mozart's opera, "Idomeneo". We were overwhelmed by both the superb performances and the theatre itself with its permanent background formed from the rocky arches cut into the face of the cliff. The general atmosphere and the dressing were elaborate. I remember deciding that an elegant black gown with one bare shoulder must have been the fashion de rigueur that season. After the performance, outside in the narrow pedestrian street, it truly was like a fashion parade, (apparently happens each year)... immaculately groomed tall, slender women in these black 'events' (showing one tanned shoulder) strolled slowly, almost in formation, their male partners a step behind, the rest of us taking in the sight. Subsequent visits to the Salzburg Festival have revealed similar après-performance parades...but never again that black one tanned shoulder affair, which had really appealed to me!

Lunch at the historic "White Horse Inn" outside Salzburg...visiting the Ischl house where Mozart and family had stayed, that glorious quite unique blue/green colour of the sparkling waters of the mountain lakes, even the so called "Wedding Church" from the "Sound of Music" film.... all of Gudula's programme for us, planned ahead with CITYRAMA from Australia, was excellent. One other memory is a superb dinner right on the lake at the splendid Hotel Schloss Fuschl (used to be a palace). A superbly set table, all the waiters lined up and at a given moment Voila! Together, lifting the silver entrée lids covering our plates. It is these small personal touches which everyone adores, and entre-nous, make me feel quietly quite proud. Lovely to share later with my violinist daughter, Jackie, acting for the first time, as Assistant on this tour. They entirely compensate for the undoubted small, and less small, hiccups which also occur....CITYRAMA or no CITYRAMA.

INNSBRUCK: Another wonderful train trip through beautiful Austrian countryside and a quick transfer brings us to the Hotel Goldener Adler, where once Mozart and his father had stayed. A charming Mozart concert here and an hysterically funny "Tyrolean Evening" as well as a chairlift right to the top of the mountain from where the recent Olympic ski jumps had occurred. After our Innsbruck 3 days, another superb trip, via Zurich, and thence along the glassy lake to **LUZERN** (so often spelt LUCERNE, but I prefer LUZERN as it is in the German quarter of Switzerland). I had secured (and paid for) reservations at the beautiful lakeside Hotel Hermitage, and had written enthusiastically in the Hand Book about its luxurious setting on the water. But alas, quite a problem on arrival. They had booked our group into their very ordinary-looking annexe on the other side of the road. NOT good! Arguing in Reception and phone calls to CITYRAMA seemed to go nowhere and truly the poor girls in Reception were not to blame. The hotel was full. I was furious, but also very upset for everyone else. Explanations and free champagne etc were cheerfully accepted by most, but a couple of slightly more belligerent ones stood their ground and refused to be happy. Next day, it appeared that an English couple were moving on earlier than expected and their two- room suite with a view out over the lake and mountains opposite was made available to these grizzlers....who, in return, had us all to pre-dinner drinks and canapés in that suite...at their expense. Sigh.......... Of course everything else happened in the beautiful main hotel on the water, lunches, dinners, lectures. And from there we attended a wonderful concert given by the great Concertgabou Orchestra from Amsterdam, with Midori as soloist. The new Festspielhaus right on the lake is superb. Two other memorable happenings during our four days were a visit to "Tribschen", the home of Richard and Cosima Wagner on the other side of the lake, and a full day excursion by boat and funicular up to BERGENSTOCK....what marvellous experiences. (I think today was also the day I lost my credit card and was so relieved to find it again at the booking office where I had left it the day before when collecting our concert tickets.What lovely helpful people there).

Because this was a very extensive tour, I had planned a three day "holiday" for us all in beautiful **INTERLAKEN**...such a splendid place on the water with many easily accessed short mountain trips up to the mighty Jungfrau. The train trip there is utterly amazing and has been described as one of the most breathtaking routes in Europe. Everyone quite stunned by its magnificence. On arrival, another of those perfect moments...a beautifully set up **surprise** elegant 11.30 very early luncheon (brunch?) in the drawing room of the pretty **Hotel du Lac**, looking out over the lake. (For me one of those private little proud moments I could share with Jackie, and an antidote to my distress for the mix-up in Luzern).

Everyone seemed to enjoy this break and we did things in small groups. There was a much advised free performance of 'William Tell' and his long association with Interlaken in the show grounds complete with music and animals and that drew some of the group. In fact, as planned, I met up with old friends from London who were going to be in Interlaken at the same time. We enjoyed a couple of outings together.

Refreshed, our group set off again by train...another superb mountain journey, passing through **GSTAAD** (of later L/M tour interest) to **MONTREUX**. Not for nothing is it called 'The Panoramic Route'...the famous MOB. Interestingly, along this route is a stop called 'Les Avants' and in the hills near here is the Chateau Monet, home of the late Joan Sutherland and her husband, Richard Bonynge. Both great collectors, apparently it is absolutely full of wonderful possessions, including the piano of Noel Coward, and another from Buckingham Palace. It is here that the couple entertained all their international friends as well as their extended family from Australia. Another lakeside hotel in Montreux, wonderful old Hotel Golfe Rene Capt, and here there are no problems with the reservations for all the balconied rooms. Everyone is very happy and excited at dinner and looking forward to the escorted tour of the **Palais de Chillon,** which Lord Byron had immortalised, next day. Such an interesting rambling castle but with such a dark and terrible history. Can you believe it, the concert here was given by the Emmerson Quartet from the USA in the Great Hall, two of the four playing half in and half out of the giant fireplace! Another much looked forward to concert was to be in Montreux's new major concert venue, the Auditorium Stravinski...a recital of Mozart, Beethoven and Schumann from the celebrated Czech pianist, Rudolph Firkusny, to which I, together with the several other actual musicians in this group, was particularly looking forward. I shudder when I recall events relating to this recital. I had taken them on a day trip to nearby Vevey, with its artistic and film star history (Charlie Chaplin et al). The public bus service between Montreux and Vevey was so frequent it seemed ridiculous to arrange a private bus and have it hanging around there for hours. It was a really wonderful day but somehow or other I got the time of the return bus wrong, and as a consequence, we missed the first item on the programme, arriving a moment or so late and having to wait in the foyer. I totally approve of the regulation which does not permit possible distraction to a performer by late arrivals. But I felt so guilty...oh so guilty! I had caused us to be late. No one to blame this time. I knew it...they all knew it. The remainder of the recital was excellent. But I could sense the disappointment, especially from the special few, imagined or not, it hardly mattered.

The rest of the group went in to the lovely supper I had arranged, but I walked slowly back along the lake to our hotel alone, feeling wretched and knowing I was fully to blame. I did probably over-react at rare times like this.I blamed myself if I felt I was letting anyone down. It was quite stupid really. It was not a major disaster. Accidents can happen. But I dreaded breakfast the next morning. To my absolute delight, some small wildflowers were sitting on my place with a tiny note, "Cheer up Roma! We still love you!" I almost wept. What a great bunch they were.

GENEVA: It was a truly memorable trip from Montreux to Geneva… one I would recommend to anyone. A four hour cruise on the Lac Leman (Lake Geneva) passing by Lausanne and other lakeside locations, as we lunched on board. The organised taxis were just where they were meant to be, and a swift transfer to the beautiful Hotel Angleterre. In Geneva we didn't have any musical fixtures other than the String Finals of the International Competition at the Maison de Radio. (I seem to remember we attended the 'Cello ones). But they all enjoy the very informative guided tours of this remarkable and very important capital city with its international headquarters and great Calvin cathedral. Jackie left us here in order to meet up with university friends from Paris. The group gave her a great send off. Jackie had won many hearts on this trip.

The final five days of this remarkable tour were in **NICE.** I have already explained why Nice was included, and I have to say, everyone was utterly delighted by their experiences in this beautiful city. We stayed at the lovely Hotel Beau Rivage and I took them through the Vieux Ville beside it which I had remembered so well…the famous flower market, the tiny cafes, the winding streets full of ateliers of different kinds, the window of the flat above where Matisee had once lived and had painted his famous violin picture before moving well above the city, and the ancient Cathédrale de St Reparate where a late choral Mass was in progress. We enjoyed guided tours of the impressive Matisse and Chagall galleries, two wonderful excursions along the coast in opposite directions… one to Monte Carlo, where, en route, I can still see in my mind's eye the beautiful pink clothed tables awaiting us for lunch by the sea at the pretty restaurant, "Le Skipper" in the tiny port of St Jean at Cap Ferrat. And the other excursion westwards to Antibes and lunch in the cafe always used by the writer, Graham Greene, who lived there. (This second trip may well have been on a later tour.) As well, in Cap d'Antibes, a visit to the marvellous Musée Picasso, where his momentous work, "Guernica", on loan had pride of place at this time. We enjoyed an excellent Chamber

Music concert at the Conservatoire and Mozart's "The Magic Flute" at the small Nice Opera House, designed by the same brilliant Charles Garnier, who had designed the great Opera Garnier in Paris.

An extraordinary thing happened on our "free day" in Nice. The evening before, Louise, our very smart and active eighty year old from Melbourne, asked if it would be possible somehow or other for her to visit her cousin who lived in Vence next day. "She is the distinguished sculptor, HILDE MATHIEU," said Louise. "It will never be possible for me to see her again ". What to do? So I rented a car and Louise, Lois, Ann and I went off on the picturesque hilly route to Vence. I found the way quite easily because my husband and I had visited the region several times when we lived in England. Hilde lived in a very charming but rather run down old house crammed full of her work...it absolutely overflowed every room. She was so excited to see us (having been telephoned by Louise the evening before). "You are so welcome...don't mind the mess. Je suis bôheme ", as she opened a very old, very dusty unchilled bottle of champagne, which shot right to the ceiling! (I noted Lois surreptitiously wiping very dusty glasses from an old cupboard as she did so). It was all fascinating. She had been the European skating champion before Sonje Heine and used to work out with her in Norway. She had had so many sculpture commissions and was presently working on the bust of the present pope, commissioned by The Vatican, and also was a great friend of Marc Chagall and his wife who had lived next door. She took us to look down from her balcony to the house just below where he had lived. It was not actually surprising to learn that 89 year old Hilde had had five husbands! "I still work every day of my life" she told us. Both Louise and Hilde had originally come from Berlin. It was touching to see their farewells. I was so glad to have made this last meeting possible for them, and what an amazing experience for us as well. After visiting the Matisse Chapel and then a hasty check of just the walls of St Paul de Vence, we quickly drove back to Nice because that evening we would have our Farewell Dinner.

The evening was warm and still as we gathered in the outdoor restaurant of the Hotel Beau Rivage. It has been altered now, but then, this restaurant was at sea level, just a few metres from the gently lapping waves. It was a lively happy occasion. I have not mentioned this before, but on this particular tour, there had been only one male participant, the other half of a beautiful married couple, who were subsequently to come on no less than four LINGUA MUSICA tours. I am quite sure that Peter would inwardly have been rather taken aback when they had first arrived at Ch de G Airport in Paris, but this charming handsome gentleman had not batted an eyelid and had gallantly behaved as such a sophisticated man would. Always ready to assist till I had personally intervened when I saw him lifting heavy luggage belonging to others at our first rail stop. I really had to insist quite strongly that I could not allow him to be the porter for this group. The others backed me up. Finally, he laughingly acquiesced. There is a tradition on these tours that on the final occasion together, everyone has a few words to say about their experiences. (On some later tours when there were over thirty participants, it had to be a minute and a half firing round the long table!) On this occasion, the speeches were lovely, some very heart-warming and some very amusing. I recall Lois saying "You think it can't get any better than this. And then it does!" Peter brought the evening to a close with a beautiful speech of thanks, acknowledging the inevitability of a few hiccups along the way, but which were quickly overcome, and praising me for all my..... "Well, you know what I mean. I won't go on!" It had been a truly amazing tour. On that we all agreed. I felt a little tearful I have to say.

My evening ended sitting at my desk doing the usual totalling and balancing which my accountant always required and anxiously checking that indeed everything had been well covered and I was financially in the clear. Final entries into my often hastily scribbled 1991 tour diary (which I have just been rereading with delight) were of a remarkable and lovely group; and at last to bed with the departure plans for all next morning in place.

Two days later, in my upstairs "Galaxy" Business Class seat, I am homeward bound and reflecting happily on a happy tour and the lovely friendships made between us all. That is one of the pluses of a LINGUA MUSICA tour... lasting friendships. It becomes almost a family. Several participants have returned several times to travel with me. I was also reflecting on the very appreciative manner in which UTA French Airlines had supported me...my gifted flights PLUS upgrades, accommodation and much more. As I write this, many years later, I also remember sadly how this airline was forced to cease its operations in Australia when Melbourne baggage handlers refused to unpack for them after the French nuclear testing in the Pacific affair, approved by President Jacques Chirac (which was hardly the airline's fault). I just happened to fly home on that last such flight and was truly devastated when the French captain made an unexpected announcement, "All Australian passengers must leave this flight in Singapore"! It was bewildering. Nothing was explained. We just had to disembark and our luggage was made available. Along with several others, another flight Singapore/Australia had to be found. After an exhausting effort in Singapore, I managed to get one to Brisbane. Then from there, had to get back to Melbourne. It seemed to have taken forever since departing France. It was not till several days later that I discovered from the UTA office what had happened. Such a shock! I was really sad. They never again included stops in Australia, going straight on to Nouvelle Caledonie. A month or two later I had to find another airline which would work similarly with me for future tours. This became AUSTRIAN AIRLINES. They were excellent and as Vienna figured largely in many future tours, were a very appropriate one to use. And they treated me extremely well (always an upgrade etc), though with not quite the same panache as UTA. Many years later, when I planned to commence a European tour in London, I thought I might give Qantas a chance to assist me. Despite having a fairly large group, they offered me no concessions, no upgrade, let alone a free flight for myself. I could hardly believe this, so took myself into Head Office. "After all the years of successful tours, please give me a good reason why I should bring a large group to fly with Qantas?" I recall that, by way of reply, I received an indifferent shrug. Needless to say, Qantas has very rarely figured in any future LINGUA MUSICA plans

RUTH NYE, MBE.FRCM

I have written an entire book about my dear friend and musical mentor, RUTH NYE, as has been mentioned at the beginning of this work, and needing to make a small précis of her life and career so as to include her in this book, presents me with a very big problem. But include Ruthie I must. She has been an enormous influence in my life and a much appreciated and valued participant on many of the earlier tours.

Ruth Farren-Price was born in Brisbane, one of a remarkably musical three children. Both she and her brother, Ronald, followed careers in Music, whilst their sister, Beverley, opted for a different career path.

When I was a young First Year Bachelor of Music student at the University of Melbourne, Ruth, (a more advanced student of our teacher, the renowned Lindsay Biggins) was already winning prizes everywhere and giving superb concerto performances with Australian orchestras. She was beautiful as well as being talented and with an engaging personality. Before long this young artist was also presenting an exceptionally good Music programme on early ABC television (in fact, in 1960, was awarded "Television Personality of the Year"). During one of his Australian tours, the great Chilean maestro, Claudio Arrau, heard her play on two occasions and offered her the chance to move to New York to study with him. An amazing opportunity, but by then, Ruth was married to Ross Nye (a remarkable Queensland horseman about whom a story has been written as well as a BBC radio program) and they had two little daughters. An enormous decision to make, but one they did. The family moved and lived in a small apartment on Long Island not far from the Arraus, and Ruth not only studied with the maestro for twelve months (when he was not touring) but he gave her the use of the teaching studio in his home. The Nyes and Claudio and his wife,(also named Ruth) became very good friends. They stayed with them on their country property and the close friendship continued when Ruth, Ross and family settled in London, where of course Arrau visited often to perform, always staying at the Savoy Hotel. In fact Ruth travelled very often with Claudio Arrau, assisting his arrangements and "managing" him, when he would have the occasional tantrum (yes, great artists do sometimes have tantrums!), and as his strength grew less. Ross also was a great support to Arrau in London, and the Nye daughters, Kirsty and Lisa, regarded him as a gentle kind uncle, and remember with affection all the visits, receptions, dinners and teas for this distinguished man.

Remember, this is a very abbreviated account of the life of this remarkable musician. However....Ruth Nye's career took off very quickly once they settled in a London Mews near Hyde Park, where Ross was able to set up riding stables. Apart from Ruth's concert tours in Australia, they never returned to live here...life was just so successful and satisfying for them all in London. She was taken up by the most prestigious concert agency of the time, Ibbs and Tillett, because Amy Tillett had by chance heard her play a Dohnanyi Concerto with the Kensigton Symphony Orchesra, and extended her Piano Series at the Wigmore Hall so as to include a recital by Ruth. She performed many times at the Wigmore Hall and also the Queen Elizabeth Hall. During the 1970's and 1980's, Ruth performed not only in the USA and UK, but in Australia, the Far East, the Middle East and throughout Europe. Her performances were always very well received.Some notable ones were four different performances with Sir Malcolm Sargent of the Beethoven Concertos Nos 1 and 3, both books of the Debussy Preludes at the Queen Elizabeth Hall, (one of six recitals there) and in the same hall, the premier performance of Malcolm Williamson's third concerto with the composer himself in the audience.(Williamson became the Queen's Musician.) In one of her several recitals at the Wigmore Hall, she gave the first performance of the newly discovered piano transcription of Beethoven's String Trio in

E flat Major, Op. 3. Authenticated by leading musicologists, it was to have been presented by Claudio Arrau, but as his schedule was already overfull, he had asked Ruth to do this. She did, to very much interest. Ruth's international career continued apace, but, with each absence from Ross and the property they had been able to buy in Surrey, and after each flight, Ruth began to wonder why she was continuing to put herself through such demanding situations. She adored the actual performing, the excitement, the adulation, the receptions abroad, but she was missing her home and all the ways she and Ross were planning as improvements to the house and the farm. And she was sick to death of living out of a suit case! Finally, there was, what she called "A Sign from Above". In the early nineties, she developed Dupuytrens Contracture, a condition where her little finger began to curl into the palm of her left hand. It broke my heart to see this situation…her damaged small but usually enormously strong pianist's left hand. The implications for a concert pianist can only be imagined. Surgery by a noted man was unsuccessful…in fact Ruth felt it worsened the situation.

Till then, Ruth had always been too busy travelling and performing as well as the demands of being a wife and mother and managing a very large property, to be able to teach more than a very few special pupils. But now she embraced this side of her life with enthusiasm and was soon in great demand at her teaching studio above the Nye Stables in the Mews, at the Royal College of Music and also the Yehudi Menuhin School in Surrey. She still gave the occasional recital, but strictly only within the UK, and also when asked, excellent Master Classes there and abroad. She absolutely loved her teaching and all the contacts she still had with Arrau, who visited often, and she became, as the renowned Australian pianist, Eileen Joyce, once told me "One of the best teachers of piano in England". Often thought of as a disciple of Claudio Arrau, the international pianist and close friend, Piers Lane, has additionally said of her that "though she may pass on the master's approach to technique, tone production, musical shaping and thought, she has her own individual approach and a great gift for being able to perceive her students' innate personalities and purposefully develop their individual talents ".

Historical **LONGFREY FARM** in Surrey is quite an amazing property. I absolutely love to be there and it has become, in a way, a second home to me, when I visit England. The property has a most interesting history, associated with, of all things, gunpowder! The manufacture of gunpowder really had its origins in what is now Germany. It was introduced into England during the reign of Elizabeth 1 and was produced at several sites where the timber most satisfactory for charcoal was readily available. These were notably the Lake District and Surrey. And there was actually production during these times on Longfrey Farm. As the technology developed more sophisticated explosives and with the invention of cordite, black gunpowder became a thing of the past. When the Chilworth Production Gunpowder Company was in full production, a complex of five joined together units was built on the property for the foreman plus three workers and their families. They constitute the later tall 3 storey five gabled house on Longfrey Farm, which the Nyes, only the third owners in all those years, bought in 1977 and worked so terribly hard to restore. It is an incredible house and property and where Ruth and Ross Nye have entertained so many of the world's top artists, and where also Ross Nye ran his Riding Holidays for children from all over the world, as well as an annual Adults' Riding Weekend. Incredibly, this wonderful pianist and greatly sort after teacher, Ruth Nye, never one of those artists who are above such mundane concerns, did all the cooking for these large gatherings, serving food she had personally grown in her large vegetable gardens. She and her Ross have always been a great partnership. In a world where broken marriages abound, their enduring loving relationship is a joy to behold. Ruth is my wise counsellor, my musical mentor, and above all, my very dear and loyal friend.

RUTH NYE has joined us on about five or six LINGUA MUSICA journeys in different parts of Europe, giving beautiful lecture/recitals related to the particular locations, mixing and sharing her charm and gentle wit with the groups, enjoying the travels and provisions herself, and an absolute delight for us to have as **"Our Famous Tour Personality"**.

ROSS ATHERTON NYE: 1927–2020: Ruth's wonderful husband of nearly 67 years, died peacefully at Longfrey Farm just a couple of weeks ago, as I write this. Originally from Queensland, this tall, handsome and extremely inspiring man, a gifted horseman, opened riding stables beside Hyde Park when the family settled in London. Coincidentally, The **Ross Nye Stables** celebrated their 57th anniversary the day he died. People from all over the world have ridden here and special services for children and the disabled were always part of his vision. But Ross Nye's vision and knowledge extended far beyond horses. Always a tremendous support to his adored wife, he was a wise counsellor and benefactor to so many. I personally am so grateful for the endless warmth of Ross Nye's welcome and his wise insights during our conversations over very many years.

CLIVE STARK
(FROM A LINGUA MUSICA PROGRAM)

After a career in Radio spanning more than three decades. Clive Stark is devoting more time to personal interests. which include Travel. Music. Gardens. and Cuisine.

During his long career Clive has covered the full spectrum of broadcasting from comedy to classical music. so his input on this tour can be expected to be significant, as well as being very entertaining.

His many ABC programs such as "Baroque and Beyond" the Interview and Talk-Back sessions. and his Sunday "Arts and Leisure" ones will be greatly missed and remembered with enthusiasm by Clive's innumerable fans.

He says."I have thoroughly enjoyed my ABC career which has allowed me to meet wonderful people over the years. many at the top of the Arts world;and working relationships with many talented colleagues have developed into friendships. But it is also wonderful now to be in a position to pursue my many further interests.

"I have so far enjoyed escorting LINGUA MUSICA tours, and in the year 2000, I am very much looking forward to being the Escort on the tour ... A NORTH/SOUTH ODYSSEY, which is a very well researched and sophisticated one."

Clive Stark is a Trustee of the Victorian Arts Centre, and this brings him into even closer contact with what is going on in the Arts in Australia.

I am certain you will all benefit from and enjoy having Clive with us on this tour. As usual, he will share with us his experiences, his knowledge, and his observations on many diverse topics.

"GREAT MUSIC HOUSES OF EUROPE"

As I said earlier, it would not be practical to describe every single tour these thirty years of LINGUA MUSICA tour activity have covered. I am choosing several to show the kind of travel and standard of inclusions which best represent the whole. And perhaps not quite in the same detail I have given for the first couple of tours. One very interesting one was a European tour designed to allow participants to experience some of the very great European venues for opera and concerts as well as the great cities in which they were located. This one was the first of three such.

On the first few L/M tours I had no assistant with me. Then, as the numbers permitted, I did begin to take along a Tour Assistant, at first, my violinist daughter, Jackie, who had studied in Paris for three years and had toured with an orchestra there. She was greatly loved by my participants, such a help for all those times when I could not be in two places at once, and for photo-copying tasks, counting heads, and being a general help and delightful companion on tour. (On one or two later occasions, Jackie even delivered well researched lectures).Then, as my tours were becoming increasingly popular, I got the idea of having a well known music public personality travel with us as **"TOUR ESCORT "**. In this role, distinguished ABC radio personality, **CLIVE STARK,** was excellent. For so many years, musically knowledgeable Clive had presented such radio programmes as "Baroque and Beyond ". He has been described as "One of Life's Gentlemen" and also one with a very clever wit. For many years, one of his programmes had been "Stark Raving ", so here we had a man of considerable and different talents, great warmth, great fun, and who would be perfect as a Tour Escort. I felt delighted and privileged when he agreed. (Over the years, Clive also became a very close friend of myself and my husband.) Unfortunately this dear friend died in 2017.

Clive Stark had already been the TOUR ESCORT on the Mozart tour and others but this was the first of the GREAT HOUSES one and "this was going to be suberb" (Clive's words).

The first of these tours was designed around the following diverse European cities, **VIENNA, BERLIN, WEIMAR, LEIPZIG, BAYREUTH ST. PETERSBURG, MOSCOW, AMSTERDAM and PARIS.** As you can see, a very extensive and challenging programme covering guided sightseeing in and excursions from all those wonderful cities, and great performances in the following:

MUSIKVEREIN VIENNA; STAATSOPER VIENNA; BERLIN PHILHARMONIE; NATIONAL STAATSOPER BERLIN; NATIONAL THEATER WEIMAR; GEWANDHAUS LEIPZIG; OPER LEIPZIG; FESTSPIELHAUS BAYREUTH; KIROV/MARIINSKY THEATRE ST PETERSBURG; BOLSHOI THEATRE MOSCOW; CONCERTGABOU AMSTERDAM; SALLE PLEYEL PARIS; PARIS OPERA BASTILLE.

As I look back over this list of very great houses of music in those very great cities of music, I wonder how I ever managed to research it all and then to put it all together with all the organisation of details and necessary inclusions. After all, I was **a 'one man band'**! Each of these tours also included lectures given by Clive and myself and various guest speakers and professors,(including Prof. Ruth Nye on five or six occasions.) And of course, in my case, those lectures had to be prepared as well as everything else. I recall that for a tour like this, I worked at my desk for many months beforehand, apart from my many other commitments. I think I must have had a great deal of energy in those days! My mind boggles now as I recall it all, by reading the Tour Handbooks plus my own personal scribbled Tour Diaries. Yes...incredible energy I must have had!

The lectures on this particular tour were:

Clive Stark: (at 'Demel' Vienna) "VIENNA, A CITY OF GASTRONOMIC DREAMS"

Roma Randles: Weimar: "MT LITTLE ATHENS ON THE ILM" (as Goethe called Weimar).

Prof. Joel Shapiro: Gewandhas Leipzig: "THE GEWANDHAUS STORY"

Roma Randles: Bayreuth: "WAGNER AND HIS FAMILY: FACT, FICTION AND SUPPOSITION"

Clive Stark: St Petersburg: "THE HERMITAGE: A MELBOURNE CONNECTION"

Prof. Kandinsky: At Moscow Conservatoire: "THE RUSSIAN SCHOOL"

Roma Randles: At Palais Biron, Paris: "RODIN: A PASSIONATE ENDEAVOUR"

Clive Stark: At Monet's House: "GIVERNEY, DESIGN AND COLOUR, A PAINTER'S PERSPECTIVE".

Some of the actual performances included,

Vienna: Camerata Academia Salzburg....at the Musikverein, conducted by Hans Welser-Most: Schubert/Mahler: "Der Tod Und Das Madchen" D810

Shoshtakovitch: Symphony No 14, Op 135

Vienna Staatsoper: Beethoven: Opera, "FIDELIO". Vienna Philharmonc Orchestra and Chorus. A very glamorous occasion with a wonderful performance in the magnificent opera house set right on the famous Ringstrasse. The interior of the building itself a class act.

Berlin: Berlin Philharmonie: This most unconventional building, designed by architect, Hans Scharoun, was opened in 1963, and the Chamber Music Hall added in 1987. This is the home of the Berlin Philharmonic Orchestra who offer about 270 concerts a year in the great auditorium.The remarkable Simon Rattle (now Sir Simon) was an appointment in....and remained Principal for many years as well as guest conducting all over the world. The concert we attended that year was conducted by Claudio Abbado.

Berlioz : "Herminie"...Scene Lyrique.Op 18, Debussy: Trois Nocturnes

Ravel: La Valse

A couple of nights later in Berlin we attended this great auditorium again. **Maurizo Pollini: Piano Recital: An All Beethoven Programme.** The Bagatelles, Op 119 and Op 126

The Diabelli Variations.

In the great Staatsoper Unter de Linden, we saw the strange and most wonderful opera,

"JENUFA", by Leos Janacek. (conducted by Sebastian Weigle). I remember I personally loved this opera, seeing it for the first time, and afterwards, sent my group off for supper with Clive, so I could be alone and ruminate about the music and the story as I walked slowly back to our hotel. It had really affected me.

Leipzig: Mendelsshon Conservatory: Recital by a recent graduate and a most interesting pre-recital talk from the Rector about the famous conductor, **KURT MASUR**'s experience in **Weimar** on the night before the Wall came down in Berlin, when he had led the congregation sheltering in the packed St Nicholas Church as they emerged holding lit candles, to confront the young Russian soldiers lining the small cobbled street outside. His graphic description of the sound of the young Russians' rifles being thrown to the ground as they joined this crowd in unification was mesmerising.

Weimar, Cradle of German Classicism, and home to Goethe, Schiller et al....writers of such concepts of Humanism...was the deliberate choice of Hitler in his most passionate and virulent speeches. A most terrible time in German history, about which reams have been written(and about which we heard many speeches), but in that year, a most delightful, peaceful and gracious small city of Art and Music. I came to love Weimar after that first visit and have returned with groups many times.

Leipzig Oper: Puccini: Opera, "La Bohème". It was a very delightful evening, beautiful singing and playing, but I have to say, not one of the best productions of Bohème I have seen! A few scenes spring to mind....I will say no more.

St Petersburg: Mariinsky Theatre; Kirov Ballet Performance. The Mariinsky Theatre was founded in 1783 following a decree by Catherine the Great for a suitable stage for Russian opera and the greatest works of foreign composers. Today it is the St.Petersburg Conservatory, named after Rimsky-Korsakov, who taught here for nearly 40 years. The performance space is utterly brilliant. In 1988, Valery Gergiev was appointed Artistic Director, and it was his direction we experienced that night.

30 Moscow: Bolshoi Theatre: Ballet, "Don Quixote ". Theatre Square is right in the very heart of Moscow and the Opera House, designed by Alexander Mikhailov and Osip Beauvais, is one of the finest theatre buildings in the world. Even for non-overseas travellers, everyone seems to have heard of the Bolshoi Theatre! Its 3000 strong company welcomes millions of visitors from round the world every year. On this occasion, (the only one on which I was accompanied by my husband, Kevin,) he was so excited to be in the Bolshoi, that he enthusiastically ordered champagne for everyone. I remember being not a little alarmed by this extravagance (and hastily whispered to him that I hoped he was paying for this largesse as it had not been included in my already strained tour budget!). He was unperturbed...so it appeared he was. It was an extremely happy and exciting experience for us all.

Amsterdam: CONCERTGABOU: Amsterdam Niew Symphonica... soloist ISAAC STERN.

This was a beautiful programme, so enjoyed by us all.
Stravinsky: Second Suite for Orchestra
Vasks: Musica Dolorosa
J.S.Bach: Violin Concerto in a minor, BWV 1041
W.A.Mozart: Violin Concerto in G Major, K 216
Prokoviev: Classical Symphony

This elder statesman of violin playing, Isaac Stern, was in great form. We had enjoyed a guided tour of the Concertgebouw before the concert with drinks served afterwards. One of my more enthusiastic guests that evening had been looking for the powder room and by mistake, had opened the door of the room where this maestro was presently changing into his concert clothes....a story she loved to tell, and I wished she would not!

Paris: Salle Pleyel: Recital LUCIANO PAVAROTTI: A lovely recital from this grand and popular tenor, well known for his magnificent voice in so many operas, as well as being a member of the famous "Three Tenors"! People so loved him.

Paris: Opera Bastille: Richard Strauss "Der Rosenkavalier "... With text by Hugo van Hoffmansthal, the opera purports to be an operatic comedy, but several viewings have me wondering. Nonetheless on that October evening, in that particular **Great house of Music** it was a wonderful operatic experience.

It was Francois Mitterand in 1982, who commissioned a new modern opera house for the Parisian people...a more 'democratic' opera house (whatever that means). It is a unique and very modern building, designed by the Canadian architect, Carlos Ott, and as far removed as one could imagine from the traditional lines of the very beautiful Opera Garnier.... the Paris Opera House at the top of the Avenue de l'Opera, designed all those years ago by Charles Garnier. It is a most beautiful and gracious house in every way. But Carlos Ott said (probably correctly) that people only saw half of what an opera house is, the part open to the public, and that the very crammed quarters where all the work took place at the Garnier, were absolutely hopeless. At his new building, 50% of the structure is actually hidden, and it is in these hidden quarters that the engineering and all the other components of a successful production take place...including comfortable quarters for the singers and orchestra. He is no doubt correct, but I have to admit it has a rather sterile atmosphere till one is actually inside the auditorium, when it becomes faultless. Architechtural critic, Witold Rybezynski, wrote scathingly in "A Blight at the Opera" his critique of Carlos Ott's work, denouncing the outcome of 'such socialist ideas'. Oh well....let us just say that the LINGUA MUSICA group didn't mind, and that the vast arrangements of flowers, pre-ordered bubbly and canapés beforehand, softened any remotely harsh lines of the reception areas, and the performance itself, followed by our wonderful FAREWELL DINNER in a sophisticated Marais restaurant was enjoyable in every sense.

I think we numbered about twenty-eight or thirty on that particular tour and as always, we enjoyed the services of excellent local guides in every location, whose love and knowledge of their cities brought them alive for our group. The means of travel were varied…by those wonderful European trains, (including an overnight sleeper between St. Petersburg and Moscow, quite an experience! First Class was named "Soft Class" on those trains!), private coaches, water transports, and a few on-tour flights. Hotels were carefully considered not only for their group price offers, but also for their central locations and their atmospheres. Meals and wines were also designed to be different and of high standard, and in often fascinating restaurants. (The choosing ahead of menus was quite a task…and always with any private dietary requests in mind). **TIPS** were a concern to me. Australian travellers were not very open to tipping and as I knew that so many of those young waiters of both sexes were very lowly paid, I always built a certain amount of tipping into the tour budget…but did expect, where practical, that others would contribute. Well……Sigh……Sometimes they did!

On my tours, right from the beginning, I had always encouraged my participants to contribute their personal knowledge and skills….to offer little talks over dinners, etc. "In this way we can all learn from one another", I used to say. The co-operation in this aspect was great. There were some elegant contributions over the years, from some professionals in various fields, musicians, doctors, artists, writers, architects, a barrister, and even excellent ones from two different people on two different tours of tales of escaping the enemy during different wars. One in particular was from Dr Mark Phoon who described how as a child he had fled the Japanese. Others, of how they had found life when settling in Australia, and of the places they had left behind. Wonderful stories… some very moving…and others extremely amusing. Some great after-dinner 'Acts' at times! All contributing to really happy and educative tours, where the element of fun was always an important consideration. I think it was on this tour that in Vienna I had arranged a lovely session in the famous **BÖSENDORFER SAAL**. This was a presentation of Keyboard Music from the Middle Ages to the Twentieth Century. I managed to find a couple of small representations of 15th and Elizabethan music and followed with some Scarlatti, Bach, and on to Beethoven, Schubert, Chopin, Liszt, Debussy, Ravel and finished with Gershwin's "Rhapsody in Blue", which they all loved. Naturally, time didn't allow for each full work as well as discussions of the changing styles…only portions. But the overall continuing musical development was clear and it was voted an enormous success. The Bösendorfer grand was so beautiful to play, but I have to confess that for me, the most exciting part was being able to have two one hour practice sessions on previous days in the official practice room of the great Vienna Musikverein, with its two grand pianos and blue velvet couches, where so many great artists had practised before their recitals. Renting this room for my own private practice was quite costly, but for me a thrill I still remember with enormous pleasure.

"ANNIVERSARIES AND MORE"(NO, TWO)

AND 250TH ANNIVERSARY OF CHOPIN'S DEATH

At the beginning of this work, I referred to the lecture/recital by Professor Ruth Nye in the private residence of the Australian Embassy in Paris. This was part of a 1999 tour designed to celebrate some very important musical, literary and other anniversaries. It was not entirely about such anniversaries, but a very large feature of it. This **second** "Anniversaries" tour actually commenced in **PRAGUE**, where, apart from excellent local introductory tours, we enjoyed two operas in great locations, Mozart: "Don Giovanni" in the delightful Estates Theatre (where it had actually had its first performance during Mozart's time), and the First Night of Verdi's "AIDA" in the impressive State Theatre. Here also Clive Stark delivered an excellent lecture, "A Sense of Style ". And I gave a recital in the gracious Bertramka Villa where Mozart was often a guest of his close friends who owned this beautiful home. This recital had been planned to reflect the various locations of our tour… ie. composers who had lived and worked in the various cities we would visit. I remember the **G minor First Ballade of Chopin** (Warsaw), some **Hungarian Dances of Liszt** (Weimar), a **Sonata of Mozart** (Prague). I think some **Mendelssohn** (Leipzig). But Ljubljana had presented something of a problem. I knew no musical composition from that city. My dear friend, Volodja Balzalorsky, came to the rescue and emailed a copy of a very simple two page Slovenian piano work to our hotel that very morning.It was simple enough to sight read….so we did manage to cover music from all the tour locations of that particular year. It was a happy occasion and afterwards my guests were able to wander the beautiful house and see the various pictures and small sculptures remembering Mozart's many visits here.

In our private coach, we moved across the border from the Czech Republic into Poland with some highly irritating/ amusing/scary incidents (it was still one of "those"eras!) and much lost time. Eventually we arrived in the utterly delightful small mountain spa town of **DUSZNIKI ZDROZ**, where Frederic Chopin used to be sent for holidays during his teenage years of ill health. Each year there is an excellent **CHOPIN FESTIVAL** here, and of course this particular year it was such an important one....**the 250th anniversary of the Polish composer's death.** The BBC had sent a team to cover this event and we had some interesting interactions with them (interviews, drinks etc) and were also joined by the Australian pianist, **LESLIE HOWARD**, who was a very amusing guest, and who agave a performance at the Festival. His programme was:

Beethoven: Sieben Bagatellen, op 33; Chopin: Trois Mazurkas, op59; Chopin/Liszt: Six Chants Polonais, S 480; Alkan: Symphonie Pour Piano Seul, Op 39; Liszt: Valse de l'Opera, Faust S 40

I have taken guests back to the annual Chopin Festival in this lovely place during several succeeding years.

Then on to **PARIS** and a repeat of most of the events as described on my very first tour, and also a most interesting 2 hour excursion south of the capital to **NOHANT**, to visit the country home of Chopin and his lover (as I have written about earlier)...a wonderful day, and where Ruth Nye gave another recital.

We went on to spend several days each in **GSTAAD, LUZERN, WEIMAR and LEIPZIG**, where great anniversaries were being celebrated...the most important of these being in **WEIMAR** (about which I shall write later). We were able to discover so much history in all these very important locations with such excellent exhibitions, speeches etc, and experience so much beauty, each in a different way.The concerts in these locations included :

Orchestra Verdi di Milano: Soloist, Mstislav Rostropovitch, 'Cello.

Smetana: "Die Moldau"; Saint-Saens: Concerto for Violoncello no 1, a minor; Tchaikowsky: Overture to Romeo and Juliet

Orchestre Revolutionnaire et Romantique and the Monteverdi Choir: conducted by John Eliot Gardiner. Schumann: Scenes from Goethe's FAUST.

Israel Philharmonic Orchestra. Bayerische State Orchestra. Combined Choirs of the Staatsoper Munich and Philharmonic Brno. Conductor: Zubin Mehta. Gustav Mahler: Symphony no 2 in c minor (The great Resurrection Symphony.

This particular concert was of enormous significance. The first time since WW2 that German and Jewish forces had agreed to come together for a performance.

See page 89 for more about this.

We finished this tour in **VIENNA**, concentrating mainly on Imperial Vienna and its great history and architecture which was revealed to the group by our excellent Viennese guide, who also knew her Art. She was very enthusiastic about the Expressionists and was eager to reveal to them the great works of Klimt and Kandinsky at the Modern Art location as well as more traditional paintings in the gracious gallery of the Hofburg Palace. I recall two wonderful concerts here that year, one in the famous Musikverein and another in the magnificent Church of St. Charles. Our final performance on this tour was the First Night of Verdi's "ERNANI" at the Staatsoper Wien.

"YOU MUST BE JOKING! ALAS, NO..."

I have always prided myself on the strictest attention to detail, sometimes overly so...maybe it's a personality defect. But in the management of tour situations, when the well- being of every member is in your hands, for me, this aspect is of paramount importance.

As a consequence, almost all of the thirty LINGUA MUSICA tours in Europe operated very successfully, with just a small hiccup now and then, almost always easily fixed, because Plan B's were invariably in situ.

But there WERE some moments! More than moments of course. From the distance of thirty plus years, I am able to recall most with a giggle or two (and some were extremely funny)...a few were indeed anything but.

One such, was on a tour which was to commence in Paris, continue to Strasbourg and further south. A beautiful tour and it had attracted a large group.

As all tour organisers AND tour participants know, as well as the tour cost, there is the unfortunate matter of the "Single Supplement",which is applied by European hotels if only one person is to occupy a room. This unwelcome expense is avoided by couples and by two friends travelling together. People travelling alone must grin and bear it. In the early days I used also to offer "Single Rooms" (which even then attracted a lesser 'Single Supplement'), but they were almost always very small and cramped, "not enough room to swing a cat", as someone good naturedly expressed it, and some others moaned and groaned, so we eliminated that option.

One of the booked participants on this tour asked to come to see me beforehand. I invited her to tea. Molly was an impressive, very likeable woman who had lived in Paris for years, had a Ph.D and was "An authority on Voltaire" (as she told me herself...which possibly should have alerted me, but didn't). She wanted to know if perhaps a "similarly educated"(?) participant might like to share a room on this tour, "saving us both considerably". It so happened, one of the single women who had booked was a headmistress by the name of Ella, whom I already knew quite well from previous tours. I contacted her and she was open to the suggestion so long as they could meet and see if they would "fit" personality-wise. They did. Over the next couple of months, they lunched, they attended plays and concerts together; they became friends.

Let's skip a little to Charles de Gaulle Airport in Paris. One of the arriving couples alerted me to the fact that "There might be a problem with someone called Molly". Apparently en route, she had been insisting that "Someone push the stop button; I want to get off!" and similar incidents the air hostesses had had to cope with. Also, her only belongings appeared to be contained in one large plastic Woolworth's bag. Worriedly, I sat next to her on our bus into Paris. I noted she appeared to be rather dishevelled, and gently pointed out that her handbag gaped open. As we entered the city, she remarked, "Melbourne is looking more like Paris every day. I must find the nearest Commonwealth Bank to get out some cash ".

I felt extremely concerned of course, but on arrival at our hotel, all the business of booking in, passports, luggage, porters etc overtook me and it wasn't till an hour later that Ella appeared in a very agitated state. "I cannot share a room with that woman" she gasped. "She is not the person I remember. She is swearing, and was quite physically violent when I tried to stop her throwing my clothes from the wardrobe". Ella was in tears. Alarmed, I rang Reception and asked them to have a doctor visit. He managed to calm Molly sufficiently by giving her some tablets,which she reluctantly took, and told me that in his opinion, she had suffered some kind of mini-stroke on the flight and needed to be hospitalised. He would call an ambulance, but at this hour and because it was not an absolute emergency, it might take two hours to arrive. Calmed down, Ella and I contrived how to manage the intervening situation.

We were going to the Opera Bastille that evening to see the ballet (**'La Bayadere'**) and were to meet in the charming lounge of our hotel for drinks and canapés beforehand, during which time I was to give a short lecture about this marvellous work and its choreography by the great Russian, Petipa. We were all dressed for the occasion except Molly, (still in the same crumpled skirt and top), who was very excited and obviously looking forward to the ballet. I felt very sad for her because I knew this was not going to happen. This hour passed successfully till the Manager (earlier alerted to the situation) arrived to inform me the ambulance was there and also our private transport to the Opera House. Everyone filed out happily to the car, and very helpful Pierre and I blocked Molly's path. Understandably, she was angry, forcefully pushing us away; but then suddenly became alarmed and so we had to be very gentle with her. These sudden changes of moods were quite symptomatic I was later told. Pierre assisted me to the ambulance with Molly and in fact she then became quite calm (the medication?) and made no further protests as we were driven the long distance through the evening traffic to the Hopital Americaine de Paris, at Neuilly-sur-Seine, not far from the Bois de Boulogne. She actually seemed to be enjoying the scenery, and remarked quite interestedly, "You do know, don't you, that I will be joining the ranks of some very distinguished French women of letters who have stayed here?" I did not in fact, and would have been quite interested to hear, but her mood suddenly changed and she began to shout and scream and I needed help from the attendant. Subsequently we arrived, the situation was explained, the visiting doctor's letter was presented and they were able to make a copy of Molly's booking- form details which I had remembered at the very last moment to bring with me. Finally she was in a bed, in a private room, sulkily refusing to speak to me. But I made sure her very few belonging were securely stored in a drawer and after assurances I would be kept informed of whatever diagnosis was made, wearily took a taxi back to our hotel on the Left Bank.

At breakfast next morning, they were all overjoyed about the ballet and wanted information regarding Molly. Today's group arrangements were in place and in the evening another performance. I telephoned the hospital several times but it was difficult to get reliable information. I had made several long distance telephone calls to her son (had to presume it was a son) who lived in some remote part of NSW, but there was never any response. This was the only contact detail on her booking form.

The next morning the group was to go by train to STRASBOURG. My daughter, Jackie, was the tour assistant that year. I felt I could not leave Paris till I was sure Molly was OK, so this was discussed with the group and they were all very understanding, in fact, had joined together to purchase a pretty bouquet for me to take to Molly. Off they went with Jackie, and I took the several Metro routes and long walk to the hospital. I arrived to great consternation, (no mobiles in those days).... they had been trying to contact me at the hotel because "Dr Molly" had disappeared! I cannot remember if they still had her passport (probably), but the patient herself...gone! And so had her small plastic bag of personal possessions, including her hand bag. (Her case, by now, no doubt in Lost Luggage at the airport). Where to start? I had no idea. I was not officially responsible for this woman, but I felt a professional and human responsibility. No one here seemed able to assist. I rang the hotel. No. She had not returned. So I made my long way back there. And more phone calls to the only Australian number I had, leaving a return detail. Next a call to the Prefecture de Police to report a missing person, and finally a call to the Australian Embassy for the same reason. I have to say the latter were indeed most disinterested and details were only grudgingly accepted! It was a Saturday, after all. But the police did try to assist by taking various details, personal descriptions etc.Meanwhile I had a group in Strasbourg. I could not completely abandon them. They **were** my responsibility. Our hotel which was full had managed to give me a tiny attic room for another night and I was just about to have a meal with one of the charming girls in Reception, when she rang me to say she was putting through a call from Australia. At last...Molly's son! But, when I told him what had happened, he just groaned. "Not again!" "Do you mean to tell me she has done this kind of thing before? You didn't see fit to warn me?" "I'm not my Mum's keeper. She does what she likes. I didn't even know she had gone to France". But he did agree to get in touch with the Parisian policeman who had assisted me. I gave him the exact name and number to call. We were no further, but I felt a certain sense of relief....it was no longer entirely my problem. I felt it was now up to this son and his family to sort out, even if I remained very involved concerning her welfare. I would join my group in Strasbourg next day.

The group was out on an excursion when I arrived at the Strasbourg hotel, to be met by Jackie, "I'm afraid we have another problem" she said, looking rather exhausted. It was hot in Strasbourg. In those days, even many of the excellent four -star hotels did not have air conditioning. We sat outdoors under an umbrella beside the fountain. Jackie of course knew all about Molly's disappearance but it now seemed we had an additional problem with a charming lady who, maybe because of the heat, or unrevealed health conditions, had decidedly changed in personality. "She rang and ordered me to come and run her bath!" spluttered my daughter, "and she wanted me to tell her which of the ten small bottles of pills she had lined up she ought take at this hour! I had no idea and I was not about to do it and probably make mistakes". Honestly....what next!

This woman (let us call her Joan) had seemed quite charming in Paris, capable and in good health, but now and from then on, had became a serious problem. She became disoriented, she needed special assistance at all times, (she actually needed a personal carer, but of course we were not that), she seemed unable to comprehend actual personally offending behaviours even at the table, which upset others, she protested vehemently when prevented from going on a guided walk tour (because she was simply not fit to do so....and the guide protested). She hated the travelling, we took turns in the group to manage her luggage. We felt she was actually quite ill, though strangely in between very odd behaviour displays, she appeared normal. She absolutely refused to have a doctor visit. Before long, when we had arrived at the beautiful **Moulin de Vernègues** in its superb park like grounds in Provence, (about halfway between Avigon and Aix-en-Provence), where she insisted on using the pool but would then become totally disorientated and need to be helped,

I was forced to call her daughter in Australia to tell her that her mother was not well enough to continue, NOR to travel home alone…that she, or someone else, would need to come to France to collect her asap. I remember the utter fury directed at me….the total lack of comprehension. Then the waiting for a return call. And finally being told resentfully she would come but naturally she could not arrive for three days. Joan could not be left alone. The Manager of the Moulin tried unsuccessfully to engage a private nurse for her, and even if she had managed to do so, Joan was vehemently denying she needed it and said, "Well you will have to pay for it yourself. I'm not!" The Manager charmingly, but firmly, advised me, "Madame Randles, your lady must not be left here alone. We cannot accept the responsibility". (This immaculately groomed, utterly charming but very precise French lady has always remained in my mind. By phone, she would call one of her staff to Reception, ending the call with "S'IL VOUS PLAÎT ", spoken very slowly and extremely precisely. Why I should remember this so vividly I have no idea. She was wonderfully helpful and supportive to my daughter and me.

All through this, I was keeping in touch with both the Australian Embassy in Paris and the particular bureau of the Prefecture de Police I had dealt with. Lo and behold, one day, the police had found Molly. It appeared she had had a great time moving from one hotel to another and rediscovering Paris! How this could have been achieved without her passport I will never know. Maybe it had been returned to her the night before she left the hospital. The mystery remains. The police told me they had her "under care" till the arrival from somewhere in France of a distant relative who had been contacted by her son. I didn't even question what "under care" meant, just breathed a sigh of relief, and returned to solving the current problem. Our itinerary meant we were to move on to Aix-en-Provence next day. All the arrangements there had been booked, including some wonderful performances of the Festival d'Aix en-Provence I had been so looking forward to. But I must now stay with Joan till her daughter arrived. Oh dear! To say that was not an easy time, is a considerable understatement! Daughter finally turned up. Situation resolved but the resentment continued alas, despite all the evidence supplied by the Manager and other members of the staff. Unasked, a firm letter to support my position had been written, and signed by all. That was such a help. And finally the daughter grudgingly was forced to accept the facts.

I caught up with Jackie and the group just as they were leaving Aix-en-P for Marseilles. I have to say I was enormously grateful for their kindness and complete understanding of my position. One gorgeous chap immediately shouted me a g/t, and another of those plus the warmth of this group worked its magic, and soon we were all looking forward to coming delights on the Mediterranean. In any untoward situation, the co-operation and understanding of a group is absolutely essential...and that I have always had.

Another tour, commencing Geneva had a problem....this time, entirely my own fault.

As previously related, as before every other tour, I rushed around this particular route, checking hotels and all arrangements (including those in Prague) and then met my group in Geneva and thence Luzern and onwards to Dresden. What is pretty remarkable about this particular tour was that in Montreux I had rented a smart red minibus and drove it myself! There had been several cancellations through illness before this tour, so we were a very manageable, very compatible small group of fourteen, and they were tickled pink that I was actually their driver for some of the wonderful mountain section of the tour (Montreux to Gstaad). The absolutely marvellous and unique Gstaad Festival, and various delightful trips from that gorgeous village. After Gstaad, Leipzig and Weimar, we travelled on to DRESDEN in our 'proper' chauffered private bus. Absolutely impossible to describe the contents of this entire tour in a paragraph or two! But so memorable for me was that visit to Dresden. A most significant and moving tour location about which I will speak further on in this account of my tours. Following a packed three days in Dresden we set off next morning by fast train with very few stops, for the Czech Republic.

For the remainder of this group it was to be a first visit to PRAGUE, so there was much anticipation. The German officials had checked our tickets/ passports etc. and as we neared the border, I was deep in my book when the Czech ticket inspector asked for my passport. Absently I handed it to him. There was immediately a very rude awakening. "VISA, Madame?" he yelled. I pointed to exactly that inside my passport, "No, No, Madame. Not correct! You must leave the train at the next station. We arrive very soon." I was horrified. My companions and I examined my Visa. Of course, it was for a single entry, and I had used that on my very short pre-tour trip. I had thought a visa-was-a-visa-was-a visa! I hadn't realised the different number of entrances had to be applied and paid for. Mark, who spoke fluent German, tried to remonstrate with this officious fellow, "She was only there earlier for four hours!", but to no avail. "What if she just continues?" he asked. The reply was quite concise."She could go to goal". We were slowing down. There was what I can only describe as pandemonium in our carriage. Everyone tried to help…everyone had advice. The blokes hauled out my suitcase from the luggage area, someone else grabbed my cabin bag, as I as quickly as possible (two minutes!) tried to give clear directions regarding the person who would meet them at Prague **MAIN** Station, "Not, **NOT** the earlier one. (Tall…long dark hair. Remember…NOT **the first Prague station**), the transportation, their bookings at the hotel, everything arranged, the restaurant this evening, the guided tour next morning, the tickets for the opera to be hand- delivered tomorrow. And, and,……" Look, stop worrying", said Mark, "Give me the paperwork. I will make sure everything is ok". I was in a panic. One just doesn't abandon a group en route! "I will join you as quickly as possible." (Personally, having no idea how or when), but the train was now slowing to a stop. The men jumped off with my luggage, and another helped me down. They were all waving and one lady called out "Go and have a good cry…then you'll feel better." The blokes jumped back on. It had been a very short stop at a very small station. I waved back, and then feeling utterly drained, sat down very suddenly on my case. The shock was very real. I had absolutely no idea what to do.

I looked around. This was indeed a very small, very deserted station.

But even small stations, if included for a train stop, had to have someone on duty. And before long there he was, walking slowly towards me...a saviour with a peaked cap and a whistle! This kind fellow pulled my cases across the curving narrow high bridge, but soon disappeared after our conversation in my very halting German revealed a two hour wait for a train to Copenhagen. Copenhagen? Good Lord! I don't want to go to Copenhagen! "But will stop in BERLIN OSTBAHNHOF" Berlin? I had thought probably a return to Dresden, but Berlin? And "OST "? Didn't like the sound of that at all. However, the only solution from here it would appear. I did remember the Berlin Hauptbahnhof reasonably well from a few years back...but Ostbahnhof? Oh well. I settled down to wait. A an hour later suddenly remembered....Brendan!! My architect son, had said something about the possibility of being sent soon by his maestro in Palermo to do some ground work on a competition in Berlin. Could it be possible?

That evening, having arrived in the rather dingy, but very busy East Berlin station, I had to think about somewhere to stay. Nothing about my visa could be done this evening. No one looked "different"...no one casting careful sideways glances. Just normal hurrying people anxious to get home after a long working day. What on earth had I been expecting? A shabby old hotel on the other side of the very broken up square solved my problems of a bed and dinner, and the young English -speaking university student on the desk was extremely helpful, finding the address of the Czech Consulate quite easily. Next morning I was assisted to call the Palermo studio and they promised to contact Brendan, who yes, was actually already in Berlin and give him the details of this hotel. Thirty minutes later I was called to Reception and there was an astounded son on the phone. A brief conversation with the helpful receptionist gave him the details of the Czech Consulate and next morning I set off, feeling so grateful for the sympathetic hotel staff, who had refused even to charge me for my dinner! Still struggling with my luggage, (which did seem to attract some curious glances on a local train) I was on my way through very down at heel eastern suburbs and on to the bustling Hautbahnhof in the West, where I tried to remember the location of luggage lockers! I gave a taxi driver the card with the address written clearly by the hotel receptionist and he eventually had me where I needed to be. NATURALLY, the Passport Office was closed till the afternoon. Naturally! Nothing to be done about it, so I had a coffee next door where I could watch out for Brendan. To cut a long story short, an utterly amazed Brendan was with me very soon. The visa adjustment actually was quite a simple (if expensive) matter and he made several calls to find the next train back to Prague. It would be an overnight one, with a change somewhere. Meanwhile, we had an unexpected marvellous several hours together, revisiting the Pergamon plus so many other beautiful locations on Museum Island which Brendan by now knew even though he had been there only a week. I began to feel quite guilty at times. This adventure almost seemed planned! It was a very memorable day.(We still speak of it), all the more so because of its totally unexpected nature.

Late that evening Brendan was rather worriedly waving me off in an empty first class carriage, for a rather restless night on this long journey. Sitting by the window, I slept intermittently. There were very few stops and the only extra passenger at one, seemed very gentlemanly. After a bit of a struggle with the change of train, I arrived Prague. Luggage, luggage, a quick dash by taxi to the glamorous best hotel on the famous Wenceslas Square, (renamed now) and the amazing discovery that the LINGUA MUSICA group had left, after only two nights!! An astounding discovery. They gave me the opera tickets which had not been collected plus a written message from the English tour guide who had arrived to find no group. I need to bring this story to a conclusion. So, quickly trained it to Vienna, the next scheduled stop. Found the group already there and upset, to say the least. Seems it had been raining in Prague and they were tired after the long trips so had decided not to go on the walk tour because they "didn't like the look of Prague anyway".(Can you believe this? But when I thought about it next day, I remembered I had read of similar first reactions to Prague by some Western visitors. An initial guided tour is an absolute must here but also some solitary flaneur- type wandering can reveal sudden delightful surprises, and the local population, since 1990, happily enjoying their freedom from all the various totalitarianisms they had endured for so long, always welcoming.) Had they not even been curious? Their guided tour had even included a visit to the home of Dvorak. How could they have been so dismissive? Anyway, they had gone to the famous cellar restaurant opposite and the pre- paid dinner there was "Ok".But when they found the opera tickets had not arrived at Reception, by common consent, they had decided to leave and go on to Vienna! "At least we know Vienna is civilised", declared one. (Can you believe this? I still can't.) Of course in Vienna our reserved hotel was full so they had had to spend that extra night in a much lesser one at their own expense. I decided to make the most of things. (After all, the bottom line had been my incorrect visa entry, so I accepted all the blame, treated them to an excellent dinner in a fashionable location, a promise their room costs of night before would be entirely refunded (grrrr!), and kept from them the news of the Prague opera tickets being at the Booking Desk,(not Reception) all the time, till next day. Reason for this was that they were to have a well planned guided tour that day and then go to a Gala First Night at the great Vienna State Opera, and I didn't want to spoil this experience for them. During their tour, I rushed off to the Vienna office of CITYRAMA and received a totally different version of what had happened! Naturally. Anyway it was a superb performance....and over breakfast the next morning, I have to say, a few rather embarrassed faces as I spelt out the facts. I didn't push it. Finally all was well.....and the tour continued without further consequences.

Then there was another tour, a rather large group, and I was fascinated by one of the tour members...a small most elegant lady, always beautifully dressed,(gorgeous little wool suits in vibrant colours), expensive "non-tour-appropriate" heeled shoes, hair immaculate, and obviously brand new expensive looking luggage. As soon as she arrived in any hotel, while the rest of us were dealing with passports, room allocations, keys etc, I always noticed that she would ignore this, go straight to a comfortable chair and beckon a waiter to bring her a glass of champagne. Shall we just call her Evelyn. She was a lady who so obviously was used to being waited upon.

Then I realised that her "friend" was doing all this for her. I did begin to wonder why an obviously wealthy woman would be sharing a twin- bed room in every location. Well, it soon became obvious, that Evelyn, though delightful, and obviously highly educated (I had several conversations with her), was in fact, rather fragile and needed much physical assistance, and in no circumstances, could be permitted to go out alone. In fact, she was quite mentally challenged. One incident followed another…one or two quite dangerous, and there were many instances causing disruption of tour arrangements. The group began to complain, then demand that the she and the 'travel companion' leave the tour. They were backed up by Clive. "Utterly impossible" he declared. (It was increasingly obvious her friend was actually a hired carer). 'Carer' had absolutely no interest in Art or Music and often disappeared from 9am for long periods, just abandoning her charge, which of course, meant she would become our responsibility. Evelyn herself just loved all the music performances and was anxious to take part in many interesting discussions, till she would totally lose track and begin to talk what could only be called nonsense. And would then become really upset. It was a sad situation and a very difficult one for both myself and for Deborah, my Assistant that year. Trouble was, she was such a delightful cultured gentle lady. It was difficult for anyone **not** to care about her. Anyway despite many really bad moments, we somehow survived.

Later on, Lindsay, a Headmaster from NSW, who had been on that tour, attended the Adelaide Festival, and whilst there, decided to look up Evelyn. It appeared that she indeed was a very wealthy woman who owned several vineyards, but that she herself lived in a nursing home receiving full care and never permitted to go out alone. Her family had engaged this other woman to take her on our tour, paying all her expenses plus large fees. Lindsay wrote to tell me all this. Not one indication of the situation had been revealed in her booking form. It was a quite outrageous advantage taken with complete disregard for the rights of others…especially for me, as Director. A situation only revealed weeks after the end of the tour by Lindsay. But I always remember this otherwise utterly charming lady with affection. A sad story.

I promise you....only one more such story: **VENICE**. A four day stop on another tour. Venice, because of its total uniqueness, a city naturally always loved by my participants. This time, a London company had made all the arrangements which were to be handled by their Venetian agent, Stefania, who happened to be a very flighty young woman, who it later appeared, was then in the throes of a lovers' quarrel. So distracted by her personal dramas, she messed up big time (as the Americans say). We had sailed to Venice from the pretty port of IZOLA, **SLOVENIA**, where we had spent five marvellous and very full days in the capital, **LJUBLJANA.** The Ljubljana days on that tour were truly memorable. So much happened. So much music. A first class ballet performance of "Zorba the GreeK", so memorable and inspiring, walk tours and several excursions (including to famous BLED), and an absolutely memorable and hilarious apres-concert dinner party at 11pm (for me and my assistant) with all the members of the orchestra at the home of my dear violinist friend, Volodja Balzalorsky, and his lovely wife, Maria.

The Izola Hotel Marina is charming and not far from the port. Next morning we embarked on the "Pride of Venice" for a two hour cruise to the unique city after which it is named. The Captain explained that after all the recent flooding in Venice and higher watermarks, disembarkations would take a little more time, but not to worry, all luggage would be handled down the runway by his crew. Encouraging news. I am quite confident at this stage, because of the confirmed, twice re-confirmed and much earlier pre-paid all arrangements for our stay here, including several porters to meet us and assist through Customs etc, and that Stefania will have all the arrangements from that point well in hand. To my mind, one of the drawbacks of this golden city, is the number of small bridges one has to go up and down just walking along the Grand Canal. Our hotel was located on this route. So all the complicated arrangements were so necessary. Boat arrival almost on time. No porters! No Stefania! Her telephone not answering! The Customs procedures so farcical, our dedicated photographer guest, Gordon Cope-Williams, photographs it! Nothing for it but to get our own luggage up and down two pedestrian bridges to where our water transport would be waiting. Incredibly, though there are two porters standing at the top of the second one, they refuse to assist."Contro de regole" they yell. Apparently the Port Area ends in the middle of this second bridge! Can you believe this? They are adamant (despite an offer of a considerable extra tip from me). Then huge Russian-looking Port Boss woman arrives. There is very much shouting going on. It is all taking more and more time, so we just leave them to it and lug it all ourselves to where we can see a large motor boat hovering….hopefully ours. Bad tempered crew not terribly disposed to help as we hand up our luggage, the water is very choppy making it so much more difficult, but finally, finally, we are off, and finally, finally, we disembark again beside our hotel, where their one smiling porter has a small wagon on to which he piles the luggage and whizzes off. We have arrived, exactly two hours after disembarkation at a point actually only 30 minutes distant! We are also so late for the organised "Welcome drinks and Chat" with the Venetian tour guide, Concetta. Never mind, she understands, and it's marvellous what a glass of prosecco and a vivacious lady full of zest and sympathy can do to restore everyones' spirits. Off they go. (Concetta whispering to me as she departs, "That Stefania! She's done this before!") The hotel staff saw all the luggage to their rooms and I was glad to have a few hours free before our happy dinner at waterside "Rafaelle" that evening, preceded of course by peach bellinis. Stefania was supposed to deliver the tickets for the following morning's visit to the great Academia…but it was closed that day! A restaurant booked for the next evening also closed, so (not advised ahead) another one had been substituted but was so far away on the other side of the Grand Canal, it was ridiculous to suggest travelling there on foot. Stefania!! Remonstrating with her in her little office beside the completely flooded Piazza San Marco only produced floods of tears. And so on it went it. This is not to say that other wonderful things did not happen on this particular visit to La Serenissima, including a marvellous performance of the medieval opera, "La Didone"...a La Fenice Opera production but, because of its technical demands, not in the ancient Fenice, but in the newly opened and technically brilliant Malibran Theatre. It was very long though! Not everyone could cope. (And I will never forget earlier having to stand in the rain in a long queue to collect the tickets I had paid for several months previously.) We had drinks at the famous Gritti Palace Hotel, delicious meals (including one at El Giglio, after walking along tiny narrow calles with memories of Cassanova, heard a beautiful Vivaldi Chamber concert in San Vidal, an exciting visit to the Guggenheim Museum, the Academia (finally), the gorgeous church, San Salute, paintings, paintings, (Titian, Veronese, Bellini, Tintoretto and so much more beauty). Overall, that was a great stay in Venice, despite the initial hiccups.

But to me, these kinds of instances are not "hiccups". To me they are "disasters", despite the good humour and understanding of my lovely participants. The trouble is, almost everything on tours is pre-booked and pre-paid. Yes, one can always demand refunds, and from highly reputable companies (the only ones I use), there is never a problem regarding refunds and heartfelt apologies should something not be delivered by the local agents exactly as guaranteed. But later refunds are no solution to present ON TOUR emergencies! Thankfully it very rarely happened. And always, always, it is I who has given my participants my own guarantee that everything they have paid for will be delivered. "The buck stops with me" is my firm belief. The stress if something fails through professional inefficiency and sloppiness is more than annoying and one always, but always, needs to have a 'Plan B' in place. WHO in their right minds would organise European tours

A further couple of little hiccups which might amuse:

Amsterdam: The doctor who lost his passport the day before we were to leave. Great anxiety. Found it, deliberately hidden **in his shoe,** next evening as he dressed for our visit to the Concertgabou.

Vienna: Night of the Opera: A highly qualified university lecturer who had not revealed a recent heart attack and problems with walking, suddenly does so JUST as we are about to leave the hotel. For heaven's sake! I sent the others off with my assistant and hailed a taxi to take her, only to find the routes were blocked and we arrived well **after** the group, with the opera soon to start. I had to leave her and run like an Olympian through heavy traffic, across the Square (thought I would have a heart attack). **But I had their tickets!** Everyone glaring! Sarah said to me later, "It was not your fault. It was mine. You should have left me. You are too nice to run tours like this". Well…that didn't actually help either. But at least she was honest enough and decent enough to explain the situation to the other guests over the later dinner. Next day I handed out every single ticket for their every remaining performance on that tour. I was never going to carry all their tickets again….EVER. Nor on any future tours!

Siena: Guided tour of the amazing Centre: I am waiting by the Cathedral…seemingly for hours. They arrive looking rather exhausted. Guide explains, one woman had wandered off on her own 'to do a little shopping'!

Warsaw: Woman who had not revealed she was diabetic and needed injections. We are in tour bus outside our hotel waiting for her to come out. Suddenly, Police arrive to tell us she had collapsed in a street down in the Old Centre and they had put her in an ambulance. I abandoned the group to our guide and raced with the police, sirens blaring! She was still unconscious. (Story thankfully ended well enough….**BUT!** No health situation had been revealed pre-tour.)

A historic Tuscan Castle, 1992, well distanced from nearest village. On arrival, dinner did not eventuate. The person charged with this responsibility gaily served drinks and delicious canapés in beautiful outdoor setting before announcing that unfortunately the castle restaurant was closed that night. A Sunday night…no restaurants open. Medieval castle. Miles from anywhere. Several strained -looking hungry faces that night. But no responsibility accepted. That's the thing I can never, never understand. No responsibility accepted.

Vienna: After a wonderful evening open-air Mozart opera performance of 'Don Giovanni' at the Schönbrunn Palace outside the city. Absoutely crowded. Our pre-paid coach and driver fail to appear, and takes ages for me to call and engage the required eight taxis. No mobiles then. Telephone box some distance away. (Oh....who but an idiot would organise a European tour!!!!) Sincere apologies from the Bus Company next day..."Our driver mistook the venue. We will of course refund". Hmmph!!!)

REFLECTIONS:

Our LINGUA MUSICA participants in general have been delightful informed people, as one would expect of people booking on such specialised tours, but even then, during the early years, when I had not thought it necessary to include very personal questions on the tour application forms, one or two dishonest ones had managed to gain access. Misleading information, positive lies, deliberate evasions of fact, so easily lead to enormous on-tour problems. And also a couple of nasty pieces of work, two examples of extraordinarily vicious behaviour towards me by one woman...never men, (though I did have one very unpleasant fellow on a later tour, who did not target me, just other tour males). I am glad to say, they were always put in their places by the supportive rest!

Well, hiccups can be survived. But thoughtlessness and deliberate evasions when making a booking by one can cause so much trouble for many. Very soon the Lingua Musica Booking Forms included many new solicitor-advised personal questions to be answered and signed for, especially those relating to health and fitness. But as I have said, during the thirty long years of our tours, such situations as I have described were extremely rare.

GROUPS: Curious things, groups. Unfailingly, by the evening of the third day, a certain group dynamic has developed. So interesting to watch this happening. A disparate group of people, different ages and personalities, coming together through a shared love of, and sometimes much knowledge of Music and Art. Age has little to do with this dynamic.... personality is everything. A pair of 42 yr olds who, at the first tour meeting, suddenly find themselves (with an obvious air of uncertainty) part of a much older group, are relaxed and 'best friends' with all by that third evening. Same for some obviously opposing personalities of both sexes. Happens every time. The 'old hands'...those who have travelled with us several times before, are of course totally relaxed from that first welcome glass of bubbly, and are ready to support me in every way. Many of our earlier tour groups had been large (thirty plus) and whilst this may be considered a successful outcome, I have found them less so, because they tend to form into sub-groups, sometimes a little in competition with one another! Mid-twenties usually work well, but gradually I decided that the ideal group number, (practically and financially considered) is fifteen and for the several last years of my tours, I would not accept more. I have even travelled with twelve or less, which is like being on a holiday!

DELEGATING: I did a lot of learning during those early tours. One very important lesson was about **delegating.** It is very important to feel confident enough to delegate. One of course is confident with highly qualified guides, and recognised experts in different fields. But beware of those (sometimes personally known) who CLAIM knowledge and ability, yet when trusted, can let one down quite appallingly. It did happen once or twice during those early days; but such experiences quickly enabled me to spot such poseurs looking for a free trip, a mile away!

TOUR GUIDES: Our On-Tour Guides were always highly qualified and experienced ones and those for the Art Galleries were Specialists. In the early days I used to go out on tour with them. However, my highly experienced Travel Agent advised against doing so. "When you are paying guides, allow them to do their job without you. For a start, you might cramp their style. Just take this time out for some rest or another activity." It proved to be good advice.

THE MENUHIN FESTIVAL GSTAAD

One of my very favourite events to include on a tour is the festival in the unique and very pretty mountain village of **GSTAAD**, in the Saanen region of the Bernese Oberland, Switzerland. It has been a favourite 'rest and recovery' region since the 17th century, but is also a very vibrant place, very popular in the summer and of course, also a well known winter ski resort. It can be reached by the utterly superb small mountain train trip (the famous 'MOB) from Montreux, down below on Lake Geneva.

This festival was founded in 1956 by the great violinist, the late **LORD YEHUDI MENUHIN**, who had a family summer home there. Though so utterly brilliant in so many different ways, he was such a simple and special person, well known around the village, often stopping to buy ice creams for local children who greeted him. When we visit Gstaad, we usually stay at the charmingly unique alpine-styled Hotel Bernerhof, whose Manager, Leon Blunschi, was for many years Director of the Festival Organising Committee. Yehudi and his family sometimes dined in the restaurant there and on some occasions when we also were guests.

I was introduced and was told by the maestro that I was indeed "A great Ambassador for Australia". (Have to say, I loved that!) On this and any subsequent meetings with this great human being, I was always struck by the way he would hold one's hand in both his, and look into one's face with genuine interest. On later occasions, when introducing members of my group, with each and every one, he always did the same. A very special man indeed. Fame for him was only a means of bringing good to the world, and believing in the uniqueness of every person. He was involved in very many world-wide events aiming for peace and stability.

On a later occasion, I had badly injured my back and was confined to my room. M daughter, Jackie, met the great man downstairs. He treated her the same way...holding her hand, kissing her on both cheeks, and showing such genuine interest in her story of our group visits. On this particular tour in fact, Jackie had to continue with the group without me till my doctor gave me clearance to catch up with them. She did a wonderful job of managing these few days. Jackie is very capable indeed, and very musically knowledgeable after studying for several years in Paris. So I had confidence in her.

The concerts of the annual GSTAAD FESTIVAL started in a huge TENT on the outskirts of the village...yes, a tent, but a rather large one, which could house an orchestra plus all the visitors. Over the many years, this so called Tent has been enlarged and modernised with every known technical and engineering resource. It is now truly a concert hall within canvas and glass, and known now as The Festival Marquee. Through the years we have enjoyed the most wonderful concerts here, with some of the finest international artists. (On one occasion, I remember Jackie, helping the violinist, VICTORIA MULLOVA backstage with her two tiny and very tired children!) And on another occasion, we were privileged to have heard the very final performance of the famous **BEAUX ARTS TRIO**, after 55 years and over 6000 performances, the year 2005 marking their final international tour.

Gstaad village itself is so pretty and easy for walking. Sometimes a band of specially dressed cows parade the main street accompanied by horns, whistles and yodelling! And also there are the chairlifts to spectacular mountain locations above. I usually try to include a breakfast or lunch experience to EGGLI high above Gstaad, as well as excursions along the pretty valleys beside the meandering waters.

There is one particular concert experience here which stays with me above so many others. It was a matinee and the soloist to perform the Dvorak 'Cello Concerto with the **Suisse Romande Orchestra** was none other than the great Russian, **MITSISLAV ROSTROPOVITCH!**

How wonderful! Zamira, Yehudi's half- Australian daughter, whom I had met, had organised for me to bring my group backstage at interval and had arranged for her father to meet them all. He was so kind, and as usual, holding each one's hand in both his own and asking each where they had come from. I recall one lady, a pharmacist, saying, "Oh Sir, I am from Geelong. You wouldn't know it." The great man smiled. "Indeed I do.I know Geelong well." At a given moment, and a nod from Zamira, I gave the signal for them to return to their seats. (During an Interval, timing is so important.) But Yehudi held me back. "Quickly" he said "Come and meet the maestro". Holding my hand, he led me through a complicated maze of canvas hangings and there was the great Rostropovitch tuning his 'cello. "Maestro," said Yehudi Menuhin, "May I present Roma, my friend from Australia". I was overwhelmed. It was wonderful to be meeting this great international 'cellist and engaging in a few moments of genuine conversation. I will never forget this experience. But for me, the most overwhelming thing of all was the enormous humility of the great man...to me, the outstanding "Maestro". And yet here he was in this case, deferring to the master soloist, and referring to me as his "friend from Australia". This was a most wonderful moment for me, a fleeting moment, but a cherished and never forgotten one. The man was so humble. I felt so enormously privileged. Once outside "backstage ", or rather back inside the auditorium, it was difficult to hide a small tear. I said nothing about this event to the group, who were obviously a little concerned, (probably thinking I may not have been feeling well), and joined in the deafening applause as 'cellist and conductor returned to the stage. It was just a private magic moment kept to myself. At dinner that evening they were all so excited about having had the opportunity to personally meet Yehudi Menuhin. What a memory for them! Another great thing which happened on a LINGUA MUSICA tour. (I didn't need to add my own private little experience).

TRIUMPHANT OPENING OF YEHUDI MENUHIN MEMORIAL HALL

Saturday, January 7th saw the realisation of a dream when the superb new concert hall in the beautiful grounds of the Yehudi Menuhin School at Stoke d' Abernon in Surrey was officially opened in a ceremony presided over by the international cellist Mstislav Rostropovich, and many other dignitaries from the international arts scene.

One· of the foremost virtuoso violinists of our time, Yehudi Menuhin was more than a musician He was an idealistic and brilliant supporter of hundreds of causes, and a tireless campaigner for world peace. One of his greatest interests was the musical education of the gifted young in conditions which permitted their musical studies to be incorporated into a broad general education. Moreover, he wanted to create a truly home like environment with every opportunity for spiritual growth as well as first class teaching performance exposure fur brilliant young students from many comers of the globe. He saw it as being a microcosm of society and with his band of dedicated supporters he succeeded beyond all the expectations of its opening in 1963. This school was one of the great loves of Menuhin's long and distinguished life.

"The most blessed and privileged of all callings is that of the musician, who acts as an interpreter, inspirer, teacher, healer, consoler, and, above all, as a humble servant. These are the human roles I would endeavour to cultivate among my beloved group of students who enrich my school, not only with their burgeoning talents but with the great diversity of their cultural backgrounds'".

Yehudi Menuhin was created a Life Peer in 1993, electing to be known as Lord Menuhin of Stoke d' Abemon, and it is here, in the grounds of his beloved school that he was buried when he died suddenly of a heart attack on March 12th, 1999. Menuhin had also been made a member of the Order of Merit, Great Britain's highest honour. Tributes poured in from leaders all over the world, and his influence is as strong today as it ever was, and by no means solely in the field of music

Mourning the loss of this beloved figure and determined to carry on the traditions of excellence he had designed, the outstanding staff under dynamic headmaster, Nicolas Chisholm and the Menuhin Foundation, planned the building of a memorial hall in his honour. This has been supported by so many influential musicians, politicians and public-spirited individuals and the board is headed by his daughter, Zamira Menuhin-Benthall, one of the two children of Yehudi and Australian, Nola Nicholas. (There are in total four Menuhin children, including international pianist, Jeremy Menuhin).

Head of the Piano Department, the expatriate Australian pianist and renowned teacher, Ruth Nye, described the glittering event as being overwhelmingly professional and beautiful in every way. The school orchestra opened the with composer / music director, Malcolm Singer's tribute to the occasion ... "Opening Rites", in which he positioned all the string players around the balconies of this wonderful and soaring hall. "The effect was astounding" said Ruth Nye.

Two of her other leading students, Miho Kawashima and Melissa Gore, played Ravel's "Valse" on the hall's two magnificent concert grands...a Steinway, and their new pride and joy, a rich and marvellous Fazioli. (Paulo Fazioli himself came from Italy for the occasion). Jeremy Menuhin performed the Bach d minor concerto with the orchestra, and there were many in the audience (like Zamira Menuhin-Benthall and her husband) who could not contain their tears. "They all looked so beautiful as well as playing so beautifully" Ruth Nye reported "like angels. The professionalism of the entire school assembly and the occasion itself were unforgettable in every way." Ruth Nye is one of the Menuhin School's most valuable treasures, loved and highly esteemed by all. She is also a Professor at the Royal College of Music, and her young professional piano students are winning names for themselves all over Europe.

The event concluded with a champagne reception, a light fall of snow adding its lustre. And the presence of Menuhin's simple grave right there beside the level outdoor paved areas, and imagining those famous twinkling eyes overseeing it all approvingly, was the final delightful human touch to a profound occasion

Architect, Burrell Fischer, and the sound engineers, had worked tirelessly to support that invaluable connection between performers and audience Menuhin considered essential. The auditorium is lofty to float the sound, with a pitched roof enhancing the accoustic, and an entire interior of different varieties of timber, gives a wonderful warmth . The hall control easily the loudness of a large chamber orchestra, yet at the same time, support the strength of a young violin student This outstanding hall is truly beautiful and successful and a significant addition to the concert venues of Britain.

One of the highlights for 2006 here is to be the Stoke d' Abernon Festival which will commence on April 22nd and will mark the 90th anniversary of Yehudi Menuhin's birth in 1916.

Albert Einstein once remarked to the young Yehudi Menuhin… "Today you have again proven to me that there is a God in heaven". No doubt he would have been equally moved on this occasion.

Roma Randles
Director, LINGUA MUSICA, (European Music Tours).

LEIPZIG AND WEIMAR

For so long known as "The City Of Music", **LEIPZIG**, 150 kms s/w of Berlin, has a most interesting history, situated as it is at the crossroads of ancient trade routes. It is also a great centre of Printing, especially Music Printing. The cultural life here has stemmed from the efforts of a proud citizenship in this cosmopolitan and intellectually stimulating town, and where Music has been of enormous importance. **Johann Sebastian Bach,(1685-1750)**, above all, is significant in Leipzig. From 1723 – 1750 he was Cantor at the great St Thomas Church (and School) and more. This is where Bach was expected by the Council to produce cantatas for every Sunday and to perform them on the organ and instruct the choir. We have been told so many versions of his personal activities; for example, his constant fights with the local authorities, that I am inclined **only** to believe what his music tells us, which is completely reliable. We do know he was highly respected both in Leipzig and elsewhere in Germany, where he had previously lived and worked and where he continued to make important visits. The Thomasschule at the time had about 60 boarders, many from very impoverished backgrounds and of very mixed ability, and Bach found he had to get them up to scratch to be able to sing well in the choir the works he was composing for them. We are told he and his family lived in a two storey apartment in the Musikschule (actually quite extensive, it is said, and with a large music room where he could welcome distinguished musicians and other visitors). He was an expert also in the construction of organs and his advice was in great demand in this field as well. From his study window, he could look out beyond the city walls to beautiful field and flowers, of which later on, Goethe was to write of as his "Eleysian Fields. The reports from those times tell us also of the gentle walking path between the moat and the walls along which were the famous coffee- houses, and importantly, this is where so much of the secular music- making in Leipzig took place. It all sounds delightful to me. The Collegium Musicum (a more serious group of secular singing) had its beginnings here. With his very large family, his endless composition, his travelling, his students, one wonders how on earth he coped. He composed at least 200 cantatas, and there are all the well known Bach works, the concertos, the Musical Offering, the Masses, the Suites, the famous 'Forty-Eight' and so so much more. There is a famous statue of our hero outside St Thomas Church, and it is here that I like to gather my groups to speak about the relevant history, Bach's work and the principles of contrapuntal composition of this time.

My German artist friend, **Katharina Rapp**, has done a wonderful large modern take on The Bach Family. It hangs in Leipzig and I am fortunate enough to have a beautiful print of this captivating colourful work in my sitting room.

Hearing such music in the historic St Thomas Church, Leipzig, (as I have done so often on tour) is like a dream come true for my guests. Often choir with full orchestra here...quite magical and we think of those long ago Bach days here. Similar experiences in his 'other' church, the smaller St Nicholas, with its exceptionally pretty green and cream interior. (Actually, it seems he was responsible for four local churches). Historical figures connected with Leipzig are all too numerous, but include Goethe, Felix Mendelssohn, Schumann; and perhaps, after St Thomas' Church, the most important building here is the famous Gewandhaus, whose equally famous orchestra, is the oldest civic one in German -speaking countries. It received its name in 1781 when it moved from the Swan Inn to a hall used by cloth merchants for their displays. The Gewandhaus Orchestra rose to fame under its conductor, Felix Mendelssohn, who also founded the great Mendelssohn Conservatory in Leipzig (assisted by Robert Schumann, another prominent resident for some time). So many world famous instrumentalists and composers studied at the Mendelssohn Conservatory including my own early teacher at the University of Melbourne, Lindsay Biggins. A classmate of his, was the famous Australian pianist, Eileen Joyce.

Our visits to Leipzig have been many, and utterly wonderful in content.Great music, walking tours, composers' houses, (where I have played for my groups several times over the years), great art and great meals in historic venues (including the slightly creepy but wonderful Auerbach's Keller, of Goethe fame.) The bustling cobbled lanes, elegant architecture, busy shopping streets and stately squares are all part of the fabric of Leipzig. Of course Leipzig, like so many other German places, did experience sad and tragic times. Just imagine the kind of extremist thinking behind the orders to pull down the statue of "The Jew, Mendelssohn"); and at a slightly later date, the East German Stasi, that despicable organisation which spied on the entire population, encouraging neighbour to betray neighbour and even enticing children to do the same. That corner location of the Stasi Museum, just beyond The Ring in Leipzig, is not a nice place. But the museum itself is somewhat fascinating nonetheless, even to the extent of seeing evidence of some of the ridiculous methods the perpetrating spies used! Anna Funder's book on this topic is an excellent read.

Just down the road from Leipzig (85 kms) is the delightfully pretty town of **WEIMAR**...a joy for us to visit at any time. But it was not always thus.

(**Just a little interlude:** *The Berlin Wall came down in 1989. During those first little research trips on my own into what had recently been known as East Germany, I admit I always felt a little anxious on arrival at an airport or train station. This was EAST. There was a distinct air of 'difference' here. And the people I needed to speak with, hotel receptionists, concert agencies, bus companies etc were anything but welcoming, in fact entirely the opposite. Resentful and suspicious and also, totally inefficient. I recall a later particular occasion even on arrival with my group at the hotel I had selected on a first visit to Dresden, where the staff in Reception were openly hostile. (One needs to remember what the British, by means of retaliation, had done to their beautiful city). However nothing excused this behaviour. We were*

Australians who had come from right across the world to spend our money in their city. I insisted the Hotel Manager be called.(There was a hasty conference in a room behind Reception). Outcome? The Manager was full of what I am quite sure were genuine apologies and couldn't do enough for us. We were 'upgraded' (though rooms not much better I have to say) and our first meal and drinks were 'on the house'. Every time I passed the Reception Desk there were dazzling smiles and greetings. Well......Mmmm.)

On to WEIMAR: Weimar has been called **The Cradle of German Classicism.** Long before Goethe, Schiller et al laid the foundations of one of the great eras of European culture here, Lucas Cranach and J.S. Bach had lived in this little city by the tiny River Ilm, in the pretty region of Thuringia, North Germany. It has sometimes been described as "a great park with a city in its centre"...I love that description. Following that 'Golden Age', the activities of Franz Liszt and Richard Strauss, of Henry van de Velde and the Bauhaus movement built around the architect, Walter Gropius, provided decisive impulse for the Modern Age. The construction of the Buchenwald Concentration Camp so close to this beautiful place broke so greatly with this traditional philosophy that its shadow can never fully be wiped away.Goethe, the great Humanist, used to declare, "Noble be Man...caring and good". It is a truly beautiful little city. I love to visit it and to introduce my groups to Weimar, but till more recently something secret remained. The guides are wonderful. But penetrating questions regarding those past days were met with a certain deliberate vagueness. I recall my daughter, Jackie, determined not to be fobbed off, managed to invite a young guide to coffee with her. Her probing revealed that he, and others his age, felt the same way. "It's our parents and grandparents who won't speak" he told her."They refuse to tell us anything. We have to find out like everyone else...by reading reports, and even then it is difficult."

Anyway, today Weimar is a wonderful little place of beauty, cobbled lanes, old stone walls, architecture, a great Theatre, painting, gastronomy, and of course Music. Concerts are held in various lovely churches, palaces, and the more recent and magnificent Weimar Concert Salle. It is a little city surrounded by very beautiful extensive woods and gardens. There are some very elegant hotels, including the now famous and gracious Hotel Elephant, where we have often stayed, and is renowned for its former connections with Hitler and Eva Braun during those earlier hateful years, (after which the residents angrily pulled down the front balcony from where he gave his mad tirades). Liszt's own simple house on the very border between woods and city is a delight. His piano is still there and I have had the privilege of playing it when giving a talk to a group.

Our tours within Weimar have always been a highlight and a great surprise to many people who had no knowledge of it, other than vague references to the historic pre-Nazi "Weimar Republic". I have to confess that before an old and very dear former diplomat friend of our family, Noel Deschamps, enlightened me, I also knew nothing other than that about this city. (Noel had been sent there by his parents to further his education after coming down from Oxford.) He had always loved the place and had booked to travel with us on the next coming visit. Unfortunately, he died suddenly before this could happen.

MUSIC HELPS HEAL
HOLOCAUST WOUNDS?

There has been quite a lot of discussion in the media lately about the kind of Germany the world can expect to see in the new millennium.

Quite recently (in August 1999) with my Music Arts group, I was in Weimar to participate in the 250th anniversary celebrations of the great German poet and philosopher, Goethe. Weimar has been called "The Cradle of German Classicism", mainly because of its connections with Goethe and Schiller. Towards the end of the eighteenth century it was the focus of one of the most remarkable periods of intellectual creativity ever known, whose major thrust was Man's essential humanity, equality and goodness. The Nazi construction of the Buchenwald Concentration Camp on the Ettersberg Hill just outside Weimar, adjacent to those sites of German Classicism, broke so decisively with this tradition that its shadow will forever cast its ominous gloom upon the history of the city.

Weimar had been chosen as the 1999 European Cultural Capital As this century closes, we are told that Germany is "anxious to complete its painful confrontation with the years of Hitler's rule", and Weimar, because of its connections with Goethe (and all he represented) as well as Buchenwald (and all it represented) has been a major focus of that task.

One of the major highlights of the Weimar 1999 celebrations was the organisation of a unique symphony concert when, for the first time, the combined forces of major Jewish and German orchestras would collaborate. We were there at this event, when the famed maestro, Zubin Mehta, conducted the Israel Philharmonic Orchestra, not only playing for the first time on German soil, but also combining with the Bavarian State Orchestra, and massed choirs and soloists of the Munich and Brno State Operas. We felt we were indeed witnessing the making of history. It was a profoundly moving and significant occasion.

The extraordinary setting for this magnificent concert at which we Australians were so privileged to be present needs to be imagined. Under a full moon, with not a breath of wind, 7000 people packed the state-of-the-art stadium which had been erected in lovely countryside just outside Weimar, in the lee of the Ettersberg, where Hitler had master-minded his further solution to "the Jewish problem".

In mind-tingling silence on that summer's evening, the hushed crowd listened to Maestro Zubin Mehta 's emotional introductory speech in which he emphasised the enormous significance of the occasion, a deliberate attempt to try to heal the wounds of the Holocaust through music. He told of taking various members of the two orchestras with him to visit the Concentration Camp just two hours before, where "...I detected no resistance. And my feeling this evening is that if Germans and Jews can be together so close to Buchenwald after fifty years, then one day soon there will be reconciliation with the Arabs too ".

The choice of the programme was an inspired one: Mahler's Second Symphony (The Resurrection), that colossal epic of grandeur and emotional upheaval in which he was actually attempting to describe the Apocalypse. Moving through anguish, questioning, despair, silence, anger, rays of sunshine, terror and mystery, it finally reaches one of the most beautiful and inspired songs Mahler ever wrote...music of a naive faith: "I am from God and will return to God." The final affirmation arrives with comforting simplicity ... "There is no judgement, no sinner, no Just man, no great and small.. There is no punishment and no reward, and the feeling of universal love on which the work ends is immensely powerful.

The atmosphere was electric, and I felt for the raw emotions which must have been experienced by those in the audience who had lost family in Buchenwald and places like it. I have no Jewish forebears, but for me also, it was a cathartic event.

I thought of my own visit, with a son, to Buchenwald some years before. I had not wanted to go, afraid, among other things, of any possible sense of voyeurism. But he had insisted. As the Jewish Mahler's music surged upwards, images of that visit I will never be able to forget passed before my eyes in distressing waves.

The gas ovens, the instruments of torture, the horrifying but well connected audio/visual history, the little mementos, the moving letters, and the heart-breaking blown-up photographs. (Why, oh why, were they all forced to wear striped pyjamas? And how is it that so many of those very young men looked so like my own beloved twenty-year-old safely back in Melbourne?) We were both shaken to the core afterwards. I believe the major shock came from actually seeing evidence of what we had known only intellectually beforehand. Man's completely inexplicable and horrifying brutality and inhumanity to man. Certainly Hitler, Himmler and the other monsters had master minded all this; but ordinary human beings like us had actually carried out these tasks. Ordinary human beings had actually constructed those ovens, had laid those tracks on which the unsuspecting victims were carried to their final destination. And ordinary human beings in beautiful nearby Weimar had looked the other way, when surely the smoke from these chimneys must have wafted over the cobbled streets of their little city of classical and Renaissance architecture day after day. Of what depths is man capable when fear is so carefully orchestrated?

I have been to Weimar many times. It is a place I have come to love. Yet an uneasy puzzlement disturbs one's happy participating consciousness in this place. Our otherwise marvellous guides and history experts seem always to avoid direct answers to direct questions regarding those terrible days, and one is always left feeling that the mental wall will never come down. Yet, for all that, it is a place of enormous cultural richness and endless attractions which continues to beckon.

A further illustration of the great contemporary significance of Weimar is that it was chosen by another distinguished Jewish maestro, Daniel Barenboim, as the place to spend the whole of August 1999, working with a group of brilliant young Jewish and Arab musicians, from which a new and very special orchestra is expected to emerge. His enthusiasm both for the place, and for this task, was infectious. His confidence in the worth of the task was also total.

We are told that the late Ignatz Bubis, Leader of Germany's Jewish Community, was very critical of what he called the selective memory of contemporary Germans. "Everyone in Germany feels responsible for Schiller, Goethe and Beethoven, but not for Himmler ('But what is the solution at this point in time? Surely the answer to such a profound dilemma is not Schroeder's one that all the dark events of early twentieth century Germany were merely an aberration, and should now be buried.

How respectfully and satisfyingly to resolve the situation continues to exercise the best intellectual minds in Germany.

If Weimar represents anything today, it surely represents an opportunity to overcome an undeniable and terrible period of darkness, whilst never allowing it to be forgotten. "Noble be man, caring and good" had been the great Goethe 's message to the world. And the manner in which MUSIC has been chosen this year to draw together the threads of the healing poultice for the wounds of the Holocaust can only be celebrated It is the most effective language possible a language which transcends all boundaries…and inspires confidence in a wholesome and noble growth in humanity at the start of a new millennium. Long may Music continue to weave its healing qualities over still troubled souls…those descendents of both the victims and the perpetrators who live together, and listen together, in a Germany still haunted by its past.

The above essay was written by me in 1999 after the "Anniversaries and More" tour. The insight and courage of Daniel Barenboim bore great fruit and the very mixed group of young musicians he had been dealing with in Weimar that year grew into a very successful force called **THE EAST –WEST DIVAN ORCHESTRA** which has been touring the world to great acclaim ever since. Alas, Maestro Zubin Mehta's confidence that what started that season in Weimar would soon lead to understanding and peace between the two main powers in the Middle East remains unfulfilled. I write this today in 2020, 21 years later, and sadness fills my heart as I read what I have just written. Goethe's famous words come to mind, "Noble be man...caring and good ". But we must surely continue to hope, even as the World seems to tumble from one disaster to the next.

"OUR RUSSIAN TOURS"

When I speak of 'Our Russian tours', I am referring only to *ST PETERSBURG* and *MOSCOW.* LINGUA MUSICA did three tours to these great cities. I have often wished we could have wandered further afield, but practically speaking, it was not possible, because these visits were part of longer European tours. However, I firmly believe they did indeed give us significant, if limited, insight into the life and character of modern Russia. It is simply not possible to describe all these visits so I will attempt to give some kind of overview of our experiences.

I remember one time. We had flown from Vienna to Moscow and Customs was a bit of an experience in itself for this quite large group (which actually included my husband this time). I was totally alarmed when my own passport was taken by a young official who disappeared upstairs with it. I stood there, beginning to feel quite ill, while the group, who had already gone through, watched in consternation. Finally, after a long time, grinning widely, young chap reappeared, handed it to me and waved me on...no explanation. Whew! (I was told later by our guide, Rita, that it was probably because I was the Leader of the group and my visa needed extra checking. "Why?"...an elaborate shrug.) So there we were, in Russia, and following Rita to the Exit, I did my customary head count. Oh No! We had two missing...a mother and daughter. Rita took the others to the bus and I returned to the queue, and there were Norah and Petra still waiting. It appeared that Petra's visa photo looked like a male one, and she clearly was a woman! So it disappeared upstairs too. Nothing should ever surprise one in Russia. All solved, but it did take some time. Incredibly, as we emerged from the building a small folk group opposite played "Advance Australia Fair"! Honestly, how do they know who is arriving? Tips in order as usual. But we did it readily there. The people are obviously in much need. A great historical introduction to this amazing city, where I could hardly believe I had arrived, was given by Rita, but en route, the broken streets, rubbish, and loitering down-and-outs were very much in evidence.

On later trips we stayed at a beautiful hotel on Theater Square (almost opposite the Bolshoi) but on this first one, arranged by INTOURIST, it was anything but beautiful. Its location was good (almost beside the Kremlin) but, though claiming four stars, it barely passed. At this particular time, **August 1989**, the Russian Banks had suddenly collapsed. (Of this I was informed the day after it happened, August 17th 1989, just a few days before departure from Melbourne!). I was also informed that quite apart from the pre-tour advance payments, all **on-tour** payments would need to be made in NEW American dollars! Utter shock /horror! That involved quite an effort during those very busy final days, trying to estimate the total safe amount needed in USD cash and getting urgent assistance from our bank. And why "NEW "USD we wondered. It was an incredible situation. My husband and I each carried, most hazardly, a large wallet stuffed with a huge amount of crisp new dollar notes in our hand luggage. Too risky to pack in our cases in case they vanished. And of course, at this hotel, there was no way the money could be left in the very dodgy looking room safes. So my entire wonderful group devised a system."You can't possibly walk around this city with all that cash on your person!" they exclaimed. All agreed. We opened a book and divided the cash between us. The varied means by which they all carried this was interesting, to say the least. One woman decided her shoes were the safest place. I remember another thought her bra best. Many of us just used two wallets in our hand bags and the men, their furthermost inside pockets. Over four days, every time payments needed to be made (and there were so many, all demanding large amounts of cash), out came the book, entries were made beside various names and gradually, one by one, my lovely helpful group members handed over the last of their carried cash with sighs of relief! Each night over dinner, we would do the sums... all was actually going quite well. What a situation! I do remember a little bit being written in the English and US press about all this, but not very much. Never got to see the Australian ones at the time.

This Moscow visit included visits to the Kremlin, magnificent churches (including the great domed and colourful St Basil's Cathedral), museums, a lovely concert at the famous Moscow Conservatory with its statue of Tchaikovsky at the front, and of course the ballet, "Don Quixote"at the Bolshoi Theatre (about which I wrote earlier....with my thrilled husband shouting champagne for everyone!). Another guided tour which excited them all was one of the Moscow Underground. It truly is spectacular and unique, with great paintings along the platforms. And also I remember a wonderful country excursion was to the home of Tchaikovsky at KLIM, a marvellous, though slightly sad, visit. It was here that the complex genius wrote his final, his 6th symphony,The "Pathetique ".A small but lovely concert was given here. We were all very moved. (Charming road trip, but "toilet stops" indescribable! I'll say no more.)

Even then, the close -to -the -hotel amazing shopping complex, GUM, attracted some, and I recall that one day when a button from my suit jacket was lost, one of my dear ladies took herself to GUM and triumphantly came back with a full set of new ones, which she sewed on herself. Today of course, this complex is enormous and I understand now stocks every existing fashion label, has cafes and bars galore, just like similar centres all over the world. But then, it was much more subdued and something of a novelty idea.

The visit to the famous Conservatory also is worth relating. Before the concert I had arranged a tour of the building by a senior lecturer, Prof. Kandinsky, who would also give an address to my group entitled, "The Russian School ", (understood by music academics all over the world to have been the history of Russian Music from the time of Glinka, 1804-1857).The charge in US dollars for these services was very high indeed and had several of us secretly putting our cash together to foot the bill. Of course I also had to pay for a translator, and that was hardly satisfactory. The lecturer himself spoke very quickly and pretty young translator miss, seemed to take forever to translate each sentence. Also, the silly man actually interpreted the long- ahead- advised topic as being the history of the **building**! Well.....you can imagine the boring nature of this hour, and several of my group fell asleep. Nevertheless, a Banquet, in the true sense of the word, in a nearby Georgian restaurant, had been arranged for that evening, and this, with music and dancing, was a wonderful and memorable occasion, drinks flowing all evening. Again, the cash payments were an enormous total, and with rather gay abandon, it seemed to me. When we returned to the hotel for our final 'Cash Meeting', and all the book checking was done, it was somewhat of a relief to know that we would be leaving early next day.

We were flying from Moscow to Berlin. All our luggage was sitting in the corner of Reception, our bus was waiting outside. Having already paid (and tipped) the hovering porters, I was at the desk settling the final 'extras' bill (in cash of course) and had noticed the printed account was considerably higher than I expected. Enquiries to the sullen girl behind the desk received the answer, "For the towels". "Towels? What towels?" She called her superior. "Stolen towels from Room 346". I quickly scanned my Room List. Oh no, could not possibly be that delightful young couple. "Absolutely not! "I told the woman, "There is a mistake". However she demanded their cases be opened. You can perfectly imagine how this lovely couple felt, totally denying any such thing, which of course we all believed. I was looking at my watch, time ticking away, the bus might leave. "Look I'll just pay it or we could miss our flight". We were all so angry with those people. As though anyone would want to steal their cheap thin towels. How dare they? But on the bus, I felt it actually might happen quite often. Possibly poverty-stricken young maids taking the towels, and the cost added to the bills, hoping it would not be noticed. What a ploy! We left Moscow, with so many mixed feelings. But things there changed rapidly. We do know that. Actually at the airport, some of us wandered through 'Duty Free'. My watch had "disappeared".(We had already had a pick-pocket incident in the group.) I bought a cheap large -faced one for the equivalent of about $ 25, just as an interim measure. The others laughed, "Won't last two weeks!" I have to tell you, so many years later, it remains my trusted work watch, has never needed repair, and has enjoyed many colourful strap changes. Make unknown.

I also should tell you of how we once travelled between the two cities by overnight sleeper train. What an experience that was! On Russian trains, First Class is called "Soft Class ", and that applies to sleepers too. The cabins for two were perfectly ok with acceptable linens, except that instead of locking the door from the inside as normally happens, the large woman managing the carriage locked them from outside. You are then effectively locked in! "Safer that way "I was told. "Much theft on these overnight trains". If you need the toilet during the night, you must press a button and said buxom carriage-manager comes and lets you out. Toilets beyond description at the end of the corridor. A reasonable coffee and muffin appeared in the morning. Let me say it was an interesting experience, but one I would be in no hurry to repeat.

ST PETERSBURG

This lovely city (one of the world's most northern ones) has been included on three LINGUA MUSICA visits. As European cities go, it is quite a young one. Founded in 1703, known as St Petersburg for most of this time, except during 1914-1924, when Russianised as Petrograd, and then renamed Leningrad for the duration of the massive upheavals of Revolution. It is a beautiful place, but has known such turmoil, war and revolution. The people have suffered immensely, thousands have been killed, and yet, for the most part, the ordinary folk one meets are delightful. It is a most perfectly planned city and one in which colour is a major focus; in fact the pastel painted facades of the buildings glow in the Northern light (and I am told, though have never seen, especially in the snow). Water also plays an enormous part in the design and culture of this beautiful city. Many canals, the Riva Neva and its bridges. The Italian influences also noticeable here. A perfect example is the Alexander Theatre, by Carlo Rossi, so interesting, and behind it, Rossi Prospect. I remember our learned guide on that first visit telling us about this great 18^c architect, son of a famous ballet dancer, who had lived and worked in St Petersburg, and of the precise matching dimensions Rossi had used for this beautiful building, 22 metres long, 22metres wide, 22 metres high, and its windows and doors, 2.2 metres wide...such classical symmetry. And all yellow and white, the de rigueur colours for classical era buildings. So interesting to learn, so beautiful to see,

It is from St Petersburg that Russia is known for its vast contribution to Literature, Painting, Music and Dance.(Just think of a few names...

Pushkin, Dostoyevsky, Gogol, Tchaikovsky, Rachmaninov, Diaghilev, Pavlova, Nijinsky, Fabergé....and so many more, in so many different creative fields. Its Architecture is absolutely remarkable, those significant domes, the design, some of it, with an Italian influence such as those of Carlo Rossi.

I have so many memories of St Petersburg, mostly quite wonderful. I particularly remember standing (one stands in Russian Orthodox churches) in St Isaac's Cathedral, listening to a rehearsal of a large choir. Unaccompanied eight -voiced counterpoint. In the stillness of that devout place, apparently the tears were just streaming down my face. I hadn't noticed, till our guide gently nudged me.

The magnificent Hotel Astoria where we stayed, the famous Hermitage Museum at The Winter Palace, (oh yes, utterly magnificent paintings from 14th to 20th century. Always at extra cost so as to skip the long queues, but taken through by our Art Expert in only two hours, simply never time enough).And yes, that Winter Palace of the Czars in which it is located, and its 'Bloody Sunday' of 1905, and also the fate of the 1917 Revolution sealed here when the Bolsheviks took over the city and the country...a story deserving several chapters I am afraid, not to be attempted by an amateur like me, but always told so well by our highly qualified guides. I am remembering also the Riva Neva cruises, our wonderful guides, Maria, (a university lecturer in Russian History), and Tatayana, so eloquent and knowledgeable, the Nicolai Palace, the Yusapov Palace, the Peter and Paul Fortress, other fine palaces along the river banks, the elegant restaurant, "Le Nid de la Noblesse "(situated in the same palace in which Rasputin was killed...well thank heavens, mentioned only after the dinner!), the lavish Davidov, and others like it, as well as tiny little back cafes and bars, and of course, Nevsky Prospect.

Simply cannot resist here telling of one guided tour which finished along the Nevsky Prospect. I could not go as I had so much work to do, but my husband did. My group returned and with much hilarity, related to me that when the tour ended, they were all hungry and looking for a possible cafe. The guide was suggesting a few further along the Prospect, but apparently Kevin saw a McDonalds directly opposite and before anyone could protest was leading them across that so busy and dangerous boulevard to Macca's! Hilarious! Some took photos of him and sent them to me after the sad loss of my Kevin a year later. That was such a kindness.

I could go on and on. Memorable on each occasion was a visit to the famous Mariinsky Theatre. Superb concerts and one performance I recall in particular was of the ballet, "Romeo and Juliet", Prokoviev's marvellous music, incredible dancing and colour, sitting in boxes, and knowing we would never again see a performance of such perfection of this particular work.

During a visit in 2004, there was something else to remember. As I said, the people one met were delightful, but there was obviously something else going on that particular year. So many institutions (like the great Conservatoire) were lacking in funds and obviously running down (the old Professor there telling us, "The money is all being syphoned off by the Mafia who grow increasingly rich"). It was obvious, in many different ways. And also obvious was that, though everything had been pre-paid to a highly reputable London-based Russian Tour specialist, it had become additionally necessary to slip various USD 100 notes to agents and guides here and there, or those arrangements simply wouldn't happen. Ruth Nye and I on one occasion, watched such a thing before our very eyes after I had been forced to pass the suggested note when something organised looked as though it was in great danger of not happening. The large denomination USD note I had given one was surreptitiously slipped into the pocket of another.

Another extraordinary thing took place one year. After a pleasant hydrofoil cruise north from the city to the great Peterhof Palace, our guest artist, Professor Ruth Nye, from the Royal College of Music, London, was to give a recital in the "White Hall", the concert salon of this famous royal summer residence. It had been arranged in minute detail months before, and double checked and triple checked till just before departure from Australia. And of course, the entries to the palace as well as the hire of the concert hall for two hours had been well and truly paid as well. The very wordy agreement sent to me read that on this particular date, at this particular time, Professor Nye, our group and our guide, would be welcomed at the main entrance of the palace and taken directly through to the hall. What actually happened was total chaos. There was no welcoming person or persons, Maria did her best to find them, but impossible. We were caught up in the wall-to wall throngs and herded through unbelievably luxurious salon after salon. Superbly set long tables full of delicate china and crystal, giant flower arrangements everywhere, small sitting rooms, large drawing rooms, enormous chandeliers, long windows opening to beautiful water views, one after another. The history being given in three different languages as we went, all of us by then in our large felt overshoes! Apparently no one had ever lived at this palace. It was kept up by Catherine the Great and descendents, fully furnished and set up, and with the necessary number of servants, just so they could bring international royal visitors here on odd occasions. (I do remember thinking "No wonder there was a revolution! "). Finally, finally, we arrived at what was obviously a small white concert hall. The rest of the crowds had evaporated while we investigated a narrow corridor which finally opened out into this hall. No reception here either. Ruth had to change into her performance dress behind coats several of us held up. Long standing professional, she overcame it all with enormous dignity and composure so as not to disappoint our recital-expecting group. She spoke about composers who had lived in St Petersburg and began to play their compositions…beautifully as usual. Then utter pandemonium erupted! Two Russian women entered from a side door and began to walk up and down the aisles, screaming at us to 'Get Out' (at least that's what we thought they were shouting). They would retreat for a moment or two and then start again. Meanwhile the true professional, Ruth, played on. During the next moment of 'retreat ', our wonderful and always helpful participant, Terry Lewis, quickly placed himself at the door and forcibly (and physically!) prevented anyone from entering. And so it went on, quite unbelievably. I was in a state of utter shock and horror, but my main concern was for my guest artist. Finally it ended, or rather, it was truncated…and the group gave Ruth a most wonderful resounding appreciation, not just for the marvellous music she had given us, but for her undaunted professionalism in continuing under such circumstances, even for half her planned programme.

I had arranged an early dinner at a restaurant in the grounds. Guide, Maria, had been absent for some time, making several enquiries, and it would appear that the top Russian organisation paid for these services had failed to pass it on. Where had the money gone? Maria shrugged eloquently but sadly."It is Russia today I am afraid" she said. It was Maria who went on to speak so earnestly and from the heart, with enormous apologies to Ruth and to us all, about the St Petersburg she knew and loved and the new forces at work today. It ended well. But it had been an incredible occasion, never fully understood, and never forgotten. The dinner was excellent, the wines flowed, the service good. Our bus arrived and I went to pay with my credit card (as arranged with them beforehand). It seemed the pattern would continue :"Sorry, our machine has broken. Only cash accepted this evening". I was again astounded. But the matter had to be dealt with. I had about half the amount of cash needed in my bag.The rest was loaned by Maria, my daughter, and another. (Secretly, I was imagining the rushed visit to a bank early next morning before departure from St Petersburg so as to make the necessary refunds).Would it never stop? Meanwhile, everyone in good spirits.I did not want to spoil that. With a small show of grace, I added the personally resented but demanded tip. Life!! Who but a lunatic would organise European tours...especially Russian ones!

My daughter, Jackie, now a mother coping with a baby son was no longer able to assist on these tours. The official Tour Assistant on this Russian one and all future tours was another daughter, Deborah Tresise. (And even, on occasion, my eldest granddaughter, Caroline, working in Paris with UNESCO, could occasionally lend a hand for a few days or a week). LINGUA MUSICA had become a bit of a "Family Affair"one could say!

Letters were exchanged with the Australian Embassy. Sources in St Petersburg were traced by them but no one within that organisation accepted responsibility. "She" had left. "She" was having a baby. "She" had moved and no new address known. And so on. In the final analysis, it was not worth persuing. I later sent a copy of the final heartfelt letter from the Ambassador himself to our guest artist and to all the members of this group. But it had all been too much. Sadly, nothing here was to be trusted any more. I decided I would never again organise a tour to Russia.

*Angela Hewitt,
international pianist*

Ruth and Ross Nye

*Frederic Chopin,
by Eugene Delacroix.*

Roma and Kevin Randles with young family in London

Detail of Las Meninas ('The Ladies-in-waiting'), a 1656 painting in the Museo del Prado in Madrid, by Diego Velázquez, held at the Prado, Madrid

Caroline Baxter-Tresise: Tour Assistant

*Angela Hewitt after recital at Glyndebourne
(with friends, Terry, Ruth and Tom).*

*Longfrey Farm, Surrey:
Home of Ruth and Ross Nye*

*Deborah Tresise:
Tour Assistant*

*Gstaad,
Switzerland*

In Monet's Garden, Giverny, France

Claude Monet's Kitchen, Giverny, France

Bach Monument, Leipzig

Wagner's home, Wanfried, Bayreuth.

*Jean Hadges outside Tchaikowsky's home,
Klim, near Moscow*

St Petersburg

*Clive Stark in
St.Petersburg*

A young Franz Liszt

Ruth Nye and Roma Randles, Bergen, Scandinavia

Bust of Nefertiti, Berlin

Terry Lewis: Managing Director, Jaques Samuel, London

A tour breakfast above Gstaad, Switzerland

Lingua Musica Group in Baden, Germany

Roma Randles on tour in Nice, France

Jackie Randles: Tour Assistant.

Group in private residence of the Australian Ambassador, Paris

Angela Hewitt with Lingua Musica group at a Trasimeno Festival, Umbria.

A Lingua Musica group in Stockholm

A group lunch in Bayreuth

At Hotel Bristol, Salzburg

Assisi Cathedral, On a Trasimeno Festival tour

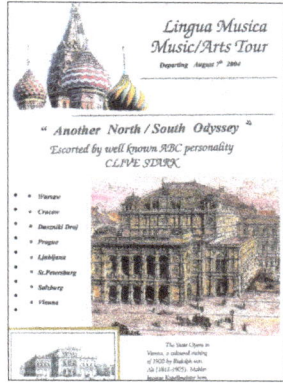

front covers of various tour Handbooks

The cover of A Life in Music, *published in London in 2012*

Edward Grieg's house at Troldhaugen, Norway

La Mezquita, Cordoba Spain

Home of Chopin and George Sand, Nohant, France

Rose Garden, Park Retiro, Madrid

Some of the Lingua Musica group in Cape Ferrat, France.

Architect, Brendan Randles: A lecture in ancient Teatro Greco, Taormina

Clive Stark: St.Petersburg

Roma and Jackie Randles. San Gimignano

Sir Simon Rattle: London Symphony Orchestra.

Roma Randles and Ruth Nye, Longfrey Farm, 2008

SCANDINAVIA

This was actually the first part of our 2000 "NORTH /SOUTH ODYSSEY" tour. After Scandinavia, it covered, Berlin, Leipzig/Weimar, Bayreuth, The Romantic Way, Salzburg, Venice and ended in Rome.

Oh yes...at least three wonderful trips within this superb region of Europe! Main centres of the Scandinavian tours were STOCKHOLM in Sweden and OSLO and BERGEN in Norway as well as and so much in between.

STOCKHOLM: Beautiful capital city set on several islands. We did everything one does in Stockholm...water cruises, guided tours of the Gamla Stam (the Old town, where we also stayed), opera and concerts in the beautiful opera house and concert halls, by water, down to incredible Drottingholm Palace and its very special little opera house (famous for its architectural uniqueness and the fact that it still uses its original stage machinery), and up to Uppsala, and all that university city and its Viking origins implied. We visited two wonderful galleries and also the Museum of the great Swedish poet, Strindberg. But I will keep this account to one special event.

On one visit, I was personally invited by Princess Christina of Sweden(sister of King Carl XV1) to bring my group to historic "Confidencen", a little opera house on her own property not far outside the capital. I was intrigued. Princess Christina (now known as Mrs Marguson after she married Consul General, Tord Marguson) lived at the beautiful Uriksdal Palace, Solna. (Internationally educated Christina gave up her royal duties in 2017 when she suffered leukaemia). But this was the year 2000 and she was still undertaking a very busy indeed royal working life. "Confidencen" dates from the 1750's and had been restored most beautifully in the early twentieth. It is the oldest Rococo theatre in Sweden. Such excitement within my group as we travelled in our private van that summer's evening through the beautiful palace park.

On arrival, we were welcomed by the then most famous soprano in Sweden, Kjerstin Dellert, who was also the Music Director of the theatre.She was a marvellous -looking, wonderfully dressed woman of great presence."You are so welcome here!" she boomed. "Princess Christina would be welcoming you herself, but she is in bed with pneumonia ", the P pronounced so decisively! We were conducted inside this most delightful building and led past the other members of the pre-performance audience to a private dining room, where a long white-clothed table was set with delicious foods and black jacketed waiters hovered with bottles of champagne. "Princess Christina begs your forgiveness and hopes you will enjoy your evening". We were all a little agog (but of course delighted....and I was experiencing one of those small private moments of 'worked-so-hard-for' bliss!). My daughter, Jackie, was busy recording the entire evening for ABC Radio, who later played it, plus further recorded moments during the rest of this 2000 tour, several times. Kjerstin mixed with my guests and was an utterly delightful hostess. Soon we were conducted into the small crowded auditorium. What followed was a brilliantly executed and hysterically funny presentation by first class Swedish artists...a baroque comedy, a parody on classical ballet. It was utterly superb. I looked around and Clive was laughing so hard the tears were rolling down his face. They were all laughing. We were all blown away. It was truly brilliant and joyous, and as well, something so very different from anything ever presented on one of my tours. At the conclusion, another speech from the glamorous Kjerstin, introducing us, "the group all the way from Australia" to the entire audience. More clapping and cheering and shouted "Welcomes! ". What a wonderful memorable occasion, and a delighted and quite astonished group returned happily to our Stockholm hotel.(For me, another of those private delicious little moments of pride I could share with Jackie). Before departing Stockholm next day, naturally I wrote most appreciative letters to both Princess Christina and to Kjerstin Dellert.

NORWAY: "At the top of Scandinavia, romantic fjords and glaciers glisten in the midnight sun". I had read these words somewhere when I was very young and had always wished I could have seen this "midnight sun". But am quite sure other future experiences of this delightful country have compensated for that. It's natural beauty can be awe-inspiring and it's a land of space, where there is time for reflection and where the seemingly endless magnificence of mountains, waterfalls, crevices, snowy plateaux and the marvellous meandering fjords is quite mesmerising in its effect. The pace is slow.This pace is rewarding and re-energising.

Norway remained neutral in WW1 and attempted to do so again in WW2, but Hitler invaded the country, forcing the King to flee to London, where he placed all the Norwegian fleet at the disposal of the Allies. This also initiated a very strong Resistance Movement and the Germans were defeated, all their installations and supply sources in the south of the country being destroyed. There were horrible consequences of course, a very long story. But Norway eventually overcame them all and regained its former position of independence and creativity. It offers enormously rich and satisfying experiences in so many different ways. On the LINGUA MUSICA tours we have experienced so much of this.

BERGEN: On that particular tour, Swissair cancelled the direct flight to Bergen.It was replaced by two... Stockholm/Oslo/Bergen, but our luggage went straight through, so not much inconvenience. On arrival we are met by our hotel's red-coated porters and soon settled in the lovely Hotel Admiral, looking out across the water to nearby Bryggen. Our hotel claimed to have a "Dress-Circle" view of the small city, and indeed it did. A thirty minute walk would take my guests to the centre, and there is so much else to be experienced in and around this beautiful place.

Of interest also was that our lovely guide, Inger, had been married to an Australian engineer for 23 years. He "had seen Bergen and never left"!

Bergen is also known as the **"Gateway to the Fjords "**. Every visit includes a cruise on the fjords from here but I shall tell you just about one most memorable day, doing the famous **"NORWAY IN A NUTSHELL"** tour. A quick trip to the starting point of our cruise through lovely steep -sided fjords to Flam where luncheon was served at the stylish Fretheim Hotel right at the water's edge, where the UNESCO listed Sognefjord ends and the Flam Railway begins. We then did a spectacularly steep bus trip (really steep!), one of those where the bus at times is moving so slowly almost vertically, that it must surely slip backwards. Exciting, breathtaking, apprehensive, but of course, absolutely safe. Arrival Voss, and its levelled out peaceful surroundings in a valley below spectacular heights. Then back to Flam and joining the utterly incredible Flam Railway, THE greatest attraction for any visit to Bergen. A 20 K steep, narrow guage rail trip, (steepest in Europe), falling 3000 feet through sculptured cliffs, cascading waterfalls, 20 unique tunnels... absolutely breathtaking, and claimed by one travel expert as being "The World's Most Incredible Train Journey". I wouldn't argue with that. After an exhilarating and extremely full day, most of my happy but exhausted travellers opted for dinner in their rooms that evening.(Jackie, Clive and I took our special international guests out to dinner at Michelangelo's, a highly recommended little restaurant with excellent food and wine. We were all tired but unwilling to call an end to our remarkable day.)

So many highlights in Bergen, but one of the most important for us is everything connected with **EDUARD GRIEG**. His charming home at nearby Troldhaugen always a must. Grieg (1843-1907) wrote so much of his music in a small studio below his house here, close to the sparkling waters of the fjord below. His music so often speaks of the beauty of Norwegian Nature. He was a great naturalist and often went off on long sojourns of discovery. We hear rushing streams, waterfalls, mountains (and of course the occasional troll hiding under a bridge!).His piano is still there in the living room and I have been privileged to have performed on it, his "Wedding Day at Troldhaugen", which he had written for his wife, Nina, on the occasion of their 25th wedding anniversary. On the year 2000 visit to Bergen, international pianist, RUTH NYE and ever helpful Terry Lewis had joined us. Ruth gave a memorable lecture and recital in the beautiful new hall beside the house, where beyond the concert grand, full length windows looked out over the green slopes and the fjord below. She chose to perform that day his **HOLBERG SUITE**, several of the delightful **LYRIC PIECES**; and finally she and I together played 4 hands, Grieg's **"PEER GYNT SUITE "**.

A little later postscript re Eduard Grieg: *It is now October 7th 2020, and during this Melbourne lockdown, am sitting above the sea at beautiful Black Rock and of course as usual listening to ABC Classic. I was intrigued by a story Martin Buzacott related about the delightful Suite Scandinavia by 'our' Percy Grainger. I had never heard it before. It seems that Grieg and he had become fast friends in the latter days of the Norwegian composer's life. Grainger performed many of the works of Grieg, who declared that no one played his Scandinavian piano music better than this Australian! Percy Grainger visited Maestro Eduard at his home in Troldhaugen, where we also had visited often, and where I had played on that same piano which no doubt Percy had used. This Suite is truly beautiful and evocative. I must try to find a cd of it.*

    BRYGGEN: On the edge of Bergen and reached by walking around the coastal path, this colourful village dates back to the 12th century. UNESCO- listed, it has connections with the Hanseatic League which set up a trading post here in 1360. Winding narrow streets, pastel coloured houses, cafes, bookshops, museums, and intriguing history. Some hours spent here with a guide always loved by my guests.

    OSLO: A beautiful trip on the fast Bergensbanen (again one of those highly acclaimed "best European European train journeys ") through dramatic mountains and valleys, glimpses of red timbered Norwegian houses as we descended to the very smart Norwegian capital, OSLO. This beautiful city, once occupied by the Vikings, was officially 'founded' in the year 1000, so this year it was celebrating its **One Thousandth Birthday**. It was initially named Kristiania and united with Sweden, with many religious and other conflicts as well as devastating fires. In 1905 the city won its independence and its original name, Oslo, was reinstated.

Later on, October 10th: *Have just been listening on ABC Classic to Ed Ayers tell of an account written by Harald Sverdrup of a truly incredible Norwegian called* **FRIDTJOF NANSEN** *(1861 -1930) who was a remarkable combination of a great explorer of the Arctic, (his ship, "Fram"... meaning "Forward", is preserved just outside Oslo), a Statesman, Humitarian, Scientist, and, in 1920, the Norwegian delegate to the newly formed League of Nations. He had also written a paper on his findings about The Central Nervous System for which The University of Krsitiania (later Oslo) awarded him a Ph.D. As though this were not enough, after WW1, it was Nansen who undertook the role of rescuing 500,000 POW's from Russia and later much work with Jews from Germany. What a truly remarkable Norwegian! He had always spoken out against the union of Norway and Sweden and was active in ensuring this final separation and having Oslo's name and independence restored in 1905. Norway is the kind of country where such unique citizens can be found. Because this was a classical music programme, I was hanging out now to hear some brilliant piece of music Nansen had written. But no, it didn't come...alas, obviously Music had not been one of this great man's skills. This I find unconvincing. A man with such extraordinary multi talents must have realised the incredible importance of music in one's life. Am still waiting. Ed?*

Comfortably housed in the Hotel Kristiania, we enjoyed a very busy four days with our excellent guide introducing my guests to the most important features here. The impressive **City Hall** (of Nobel Peace Prize fame), the **Munch Museum** (everyone seemed already to have known the presence here of his famous painting, "The Scream"), the Museum of the famous Norwegian writer/playwright, **Henrik Ibsen,** and the extensive and very moving **Vigeland Sculpture Park**, where representations of the stages of human life, from babyhood, through lithesome twenties, thirties and onwards, till sympathetic images of old age, are spaced out in an arresting pattern. A very memorable experience. A beautiful performance in the Oslo Konzerthaus (and one at the amazing Oslo Opera House were included in a later visit. The latter huge building with its angled exterior encased in marble from Carrera, Italy, and white granite, appears to just rise from the sea.) We also enjoyed lunch above the city at spectacular Holmkolen (beside the famous ski jump) and a dinner in the lovely Theatrekallen Restaurant.

A highlight in Oslo 2000 was a beautiful recital given by Ruth Nye at the impressive **Barrett Due Musikinstitut**, at the invitation of its Director and which was attended by the Australian Consul, Anne-Grete Norderde, who joined us for lunch afterwards. She was absolutely delightful and gave us the news of the very recent appointment of Simone Young as Conductor of the Bergen Philharmonic, the oldest orchestra in Europe. Ruth's moving recital here was from Franz Liszt's last chapter. She included some from his Third Year of **"Les Pelerinages", Klavierstuckes** and **Nocturnes**, and the so beautiful **Romance Oubliée**. Two of us in the audience were reduced to slight tears, having both lost our husbands early that year. We said goodbye to Ruth in Oslo.

This wonderful visit to Scandinavia ended next day when we boarded the elegant ship, "Princess Raghilde" for a beautiful day cruise and overnight crossing to Kiel, Northern Germany. It was a truly exciting experience for this group, beautiful mountain and coastal scenes as we sailed by, and finishing with an enjoyable evening dinner and a comfortable night in cabins for two. 9.30 next morning saw us disembarking and joining our bus parked so conveniently right beside the ship, for our journey to Berlin. Everything had fallen into place so satisfactorily during this Scandinavian trip. Jackie and I were very happy. Clive was his usual happy calm self. All was well. Everyone rested and looking toward their next experiences. So many new tour locations and events still to be negotiated. Bus trips for me were heaven-sent opportunities to tick off and check tickets and paperwork. Always masses of paperwork! In those days, we could not have imagined how more streamlined it would all later become through the advent of laptops.

This particular tour continued to Berlin, the Romantic Way (including **Oberammagau** for the once every ten years, Passion Play), Salzburg and Vienna.

2001
"A FRENCH / ITALIAN RHAPSODY"

About 8am, August 31st, **1997,** and I am just seated, ready to fly to Paris from London. A French gentleman has taken his seat beside me and opens his newspaper. We both gasp. Very large black headlines, "DIANA MORT"! I was remembering this terrible event as once again, this time, September 11th, **2001,** my plane was coming in to land at Charles de Gaulle Airport. The usual busy arrival and taxi to my hotel. Some unpacking, then propped up on my bed, I was idly leafing through some paperwork for this tour, to commence when my group arrived next day. I planned a short rest then a pleasant "Hello again Paris!" solo stroll. The phone rang. It was Florence, my delightful French friend with whom I was to dine that evening. "Are you watching television?" she asked. I wondered why anyone from Australia just arrived again in her favourite European city would be watching television! "I think you should" advised Florence. Well, what can one say? The horror, the disbelief, the overriding incredulity, the fear. There is absolutely no need to describe any further. It was just as we all felt. My first impulse was to ring my family...but of course they would be asleep. The Hotel Manager came to my door to enquire if I was ok. She brought me some tea! She also brought a useful typed sheet of information for hotel guests regarding the international events. Florence and I did meet that evening and as we walked along the streets of the Latin Quarter, one could see the shock and grief in the faces of others, both French and visitors. It made no difference.

My Australian group duly arrived next day, to be met and brought to our hotel by my oft- used charming Parisian guide, Frank. Several from London and elsewhere arrived independently by taxis. The Welcome Dinner that evening did happen as planned, but in a stunned kind of way. One of my guests, had heard the news just before leaving for Melbourne Airport, feeling the flight might well be cancelled. Others actually first heard the news in- flight, which was probably worse. Anyway, no matter how it was, and how I felt, somehow I had to make certain this Parisian sector of the tour remained in place. Amazingly, nothing was actually cancelled, but there were several disturbances and enforced slight changes of plan. I recall particularly, when I was about to hand the group over to our Art Guide at the Musée d'Orsay, it was announced (in two different languages) there would be a three minute silence. This was extremely moving. Afterwards, as I walked away to check other arrangements, I noticed many small shocked groups of Americans huddled together, others like myself, stopping briefly just to say "So so sorry". There was this concerted air of bewilderment. All flights in and out of America had been cancelled. Apart from anything else, there would have been so many practical changes now to put in place. I stopped for a coffee en route in the Rue Belchasse and shared a table with a young couple from New York. They were in tears and wanting to share their feelings with this total stranger. Actually, that day, I don't think anyone was a "total stranger".Everyone was trying, in some kind of fashion, just to comprehend and to comfort.

The group Parisian arrangements went ahead, a really wonderful "Rigoletto" at the Opera House, two beautiful concerts (including a Bach one in the upper chapel of the Sainte Chapelle with its superb stained glass windows, given by a Russian orchestra from Minsk), a talk by Florence about "Living in Paris Today ", some beautiful meals in delightful restaurants, galleries. But I was also conscious of everyone's need quickly to get back to their rooms to watch the latest News. I felt much the same. One felt the world would never be the same. Bush announces "America is At War".

Anyway, this 2001 tour moved on, by air from Orly Airport, to **Aix-en-Provence**, which is always so much enjoyed by my groups. A lovely chamber music concert, a guided visit to the charming old atelier of Paul Cezanne, lunch at the historic "Deux Garcons" restaurant and a couple of interesting lectures, one by a barrister friend of mine from London, who spoke about her work in relation to Children and the Law. In addition, I had arranged a special dinner in a nearby chateau where the topic for the evening was "The Night". Each had been asked to recite a few lines or a verse from a poem about the Night. This went off very well indeed, as we enjoyed a beautifully presented meal and excellent local wines. It finished with a short recital from me of piano works related to The Night.

By then I was noticing one particular chap who often behaved very rudely, feigning boredom through speeches, snoring loudly through performances...a Mr Parkes. I don't know how his wife tolerated this behaviour. What on earth was such an odious fellow doing on such a tour as this?

The following day a wonderful excursion through some beautiful Provencal towns and villages. Avignon, Les Baux, Pont du Gard, St. Remy, etc, with Sebastienne and Simonella (such colourful names!) and through their informative talks en route, making it all come alive for them. They included stops at special places for lunch and coffees, and the group arrived back at the hotel very happy and full of stories to tell me.

We continue down to the Mediterranean, and along a winding route to St. Paul de Vence for lunch and some visiting of this gorgeous small elevated walled town, before visiting the Chapel du Rosaire at nearby Vence. Somehow our experience in Henri Matisse's beautifully designed chapel was especially profound that day as we sat in silence and thought about the tragedies which had occurred. Finally arrived in Nice. So far on this tour, my usual assistant, my daughter, Jackie, because of important commitments in Australia, had not been able to join us. She arrives now as also does **RUTH NYE** from London, who will give a lecture and recital of **DEBUSSY** here. This is a very special occasion and afterwards we sit out on the terrace of the Hotel Westminster opposite the sea and cocktails are served. All enjoy this sophisticated setting tremendously. Included here also the usual guided visits in and out of beautiful Nice over the following days.

We are then scheduled to go by a splendid train trip from Nice, across the Italian border to **ASCONA** right at the top of the Italian Lakes, for a concert of the annual Ascona Music Festival to be conducted by Sir Neville Mariner. It is a most delightful trip with lunch on board. But en route, an American passenger has a heart attack. A doctor from among the passengers is called. He attends to this poor fellow for some time, till the train is stopped at a small place where an ambulance is waiting and he is taken off. This is something most certainly not scheduled and we are held up for a quite considerable time, causing a much later than planned arrival. There is a very hectic gallop to drop things off at hotel and get to the small restaurant beside the concert hall, where Sir Neville and Lady Mariner had graciously agreed to meet us. Finally Sir Neville must go to his orchestra but his charming wife stays to dine with the group, and after the concert, Sir Neville joins as well. A great privilege. And in what an absolutely beautiful location! Ascona, with its pretty colourful buildings, right there at the top of the Lago Maggiore, where Switzerland joins Italy. Ruth gives a most interesting talk here on 'The Specialist Music School' (actually referring more directly to the Yehudi Menuhin School in Surrey where she is Professor of Piano).

We reluctantly leave beautiful Ascona and travel by water, stopping at the lovely Brissago Islands, to **STRESA**, further along the Lago Maggiore, which also has a large annual musical festival, but this time one of the two concerts arranged was cancelled at the last moment and our glamorous Hotel Bristol right on the water front was only half full. We were told they had expected to be full as usual, but (with a sad shake of the head) "No, the people from America and elsewhere did not turn up". They were marvellously kind to us and Ruth gave an excellent lecture / recital on **SCHUBERT** which saved the day. It was already obvious that much had been disrupted in various places and we decided to get to Milano as quickly as possible. Even then, many hold ups en route. The great Duomo, The La Scala Museum (a quite amazing place full of musical history), a farewell Lunch for Ruth, (who flew off from Milano), and finally the opera concert in Teatro La Scala itself. It is very late when we arrive at our sweet hotel in **San Gimignano**. I had planned a very pleasant restful five days here. Restful yes, but with so much to discover about this fascinating little city and its distinctive towers. There were also to be several day excursions, using San Gimignano as our base. Erica, our excellent local guide, was absolutely marvellous when two different people engaged in running pre-arranged tours cancelled because of family associations with the Twin Towers tragedy. This was the very last thing one might expect in little San Gimignano! A lot of stressful behind-the-scenes re-organising had to be done. A full day tour to FLORENCE had already been put in place and wonderful Erica took over this. She did a very good guided tour of this most wonderful city centre and Jackie had arranged lunch at the sophisticated Hotel Gallery Art. The opera, "Don Pasquale "was excellent, but again, the theatre half empty. And again, I am told it **had** been a full house, but "post tragedy", so few of the reservations had been taken up. Barrister friend, Maureen Mullally, from London leaves us here for a Conference elsewhere.

Visits to Radda and Greve, hastily arranged by Erica were great experiences for the group plus a full day tour to Volterra, with its Etruscan Museum, the Roman Theatre ruins and so much more. In the end, it all worked out. But truly, no one knows what sometimes goes on behind the scenes! It can be totally exhausting.

We are continuing this wonderful tour with six days in **SICILY** and the most convenient way to get there from here is a flight from Pisa to Catania. This we take, and are met by Aurelia, our guide, who is efficient and very amusing. My son, Brendan, who has been working as an architect in Palermo for several years also arrives. Brendan proves to be an excellent, very knowledgeable and amusing guide. We are staying in the most beautiful hotel in Taormino...it is quite over the top. Here he gives a great lecture, and during the following cocktail party, tells some very amusing stories of life in Sicily (and also, alas, about his mother!). He gives another excellent lecture inside the fantastic ruins of the Teatro Greco, and directs several visits along spectacular routes including a beautiful one to Cefalu. Finally we are in Palermo and are joined by Brendan's maestro, Dr. Roberto Collova, who shows some spectacular images of this amazing city. It is at the pre-dinner reception here, that the questionable Mr. Parkes makes some very audible sexist remarks about another male member of the group. I am on the point of asking him to leave, but swallow hard and don't. Today of course I would. But I guess then I didn't have quite that particular confidence, and truly, after all the pre-Sicily adjustments which had had to be made, I was rather exhausted and just didn't want what may have turned into a nasty scene. He settled down once several of the group shushed him up.

During the next days, explorations in Palermo and brilliant trips to Agrigento, Segesta and Erice, one of the most charming of mountain villages, and where its cathedral is possibly the prettiest I have ever seen. Brendan introduced us to a highly learned and delightful official guide, Pina, and together they had such wonderful history and stories to relate to my group on several further explorations. It is sad to farewell them both when we depart for ROME. The extra security measures at both airports are very noticeable.

The Rome few days are very full. We stay in the charming Hotel Nazionale, situated on the Piazza Montecitorio, the same piazza as the Italian Parliament, and where I have brought groups several times. The usual guided tours of the city, plus the separate Ancient City tour, which includes the Vatican etc. I have also arranged an address to be given by Australian journalist and broadcaster, Desmond O'Grady, who speaks about the Vatican and its position in Modern Day Rome. One symphony concert and a ballet performance at the great Teatro dell'Opera are included, but I am not at all well here in Rome and miss all the outings. In fact the hotel calls a doctor and they kindly send a young assistant to a pharmacy for the medications he prescribes. (The Parkes thankfully have left early and flown on elsewhere).

A Farewell Dinner in the hotel's restaurant brings this long and most significant tour to a close. We gather beside the private bus which will take them to the airport (I am staying on with Jackie another two days for recovery before further research elsewhere), and most of us feel quite astonished that despite the enormity of such an international tragedy, this tour did survive.There were a few occasions when the effects were most definitely felt. But on the whole, the world already, it seemed, was continuing just as before. I think, for me, this particular tour had been more exhausting than most. I felt particularly drained, emotionally as much as physically. It is absolutely wonderful to be doing such things and sharing knowledge and great music and art with others. I do love it so much. But just sometimes (behind the scenes) it can be difficult and the most difficult part of all is keeping that fact hidden from the others! One could call it a balancing act.

As I look back over that particularly difficult tour, and in fact all of them, I realise that from the first meeting with each group, one is actually, in a certain sense, 'performing'. You can be relaxed and really enjoying your group and what you are doing. But, at all times, the full responsibility remains. Whatever happens, "The show must go on ". Perhaps this is the same in any professional situation. Thankfully, over the thirty years, extremely difficult situations have been very rare. But even when a tour is running perfectly, the need to appear totally relaxed and fully "in control" at all times is an ongoing requirement. It needs practice. It needs experience. It needs commitment. And, above all, it needs the support and co-operation of one's group. This I am very grateful always to have had, and to have felt confident that most will call any possible stirrers into line. My groups have been absolutely wonderful.

"A FEAST OF WINE AND MUSIC"

Escorted by well known wine identity, CHRISTOPHER BARNES, AM.

It is a co-incidence that two couples, vignerons, Judy and Gordon Cope-Williams, and Christopher and Kathie Barnes, had come on a couple of my previous tours. Over breakfast one morning, while we were all staying after a birthday celebration the evening before at the home of the Cope-Williams on their vineyard in Romsey, Victoria, Kathie put forward the suggestion, "Why don't we do a combined Wine and Music tour next year?" This suggestion was taken up excitedly by the others. What a combination! And after a little hesitation, and once Chris assured me he would plan and put into place all the WINE part of such a tour, I agreed. I would do what I usually do, whilst Chris would create the specialist Wine components of the tour. It sounded a very workable plan.

So the following September saw us, by mutual agreement, commencing this tour in beautiful **LJUBLJANA,** a place I love. It was great to be back here again. Such a pretty little city with everything a larger one has, and more. Jose Plecnic, the brilliant architect who was born in Ljubljana in 1872, had, over three decades, absolutely transformed the place. After a sad period of war and division, now a bustling little city of universities, thousands of students, many little coffee bars and restaurants either side of its picturesque central river with its triple bridge, wide staircases, tall pillars, beautiful squares and wonderful buildings. It is a city which is not only heavily invested in business, but also greatly in the Arts. Music, Dance and Drama are all very important here, and there is a very significant annual Music Festival every September. We had arrived at just the right time for some wonderful performances. High above the city, in the old castle, we enjoyed a brilliant concert by the celebrated Amael Chamber Trio (**Mozart Piano Trio K548; Schubert's beautiful 'Notturno"in E flat major;** and the great **Beethoven "Archduke Trio"**). It was a superb experience, and seeing the city lights below from the ramparts of the ancient castle adding to the delight. This was all made possible by my great friend, international violinist, **VOLODJA BALZALORSKY**, who is Head of the Music Department at the University of Slovenia. We also attended a wonderful concert given by the Slovenian Symphony Orchestra and an amazing and very moving performance of **"Zorba the Greek"**, a wonderful surprise from the Maribor Ballet. (Richard Tognetti was still Orchestra Director in Maribor during this time). It was truly memorable in every way, brilliant dancing, brilliant acting and this so familiar music of Theordorakis we had never imagined being used in such a creative way.

MOZART'S 250Th BIRTHDAY: (1756 – 1791)

In Ljubljana that year we were also celebrating the **birthday** (this time) of Mozart. Brilliant young French pianist, **EMMANUEL DESPAX** had agreed to give a full recital for us (an impressive programme: **Busoni: Carmen Fantasy; Liszt Ballade No 3, the entire Schumann Symphonic Etudes**), and also to participate next day when we celebrated Mozart with an excellent BBC DVD, a talk by Deborah about Cosima Mozart (dispelling so many of the ridiculous tales surrounding her). Emmanuel would then play Mozart's beautiful and perhaps most well known **Sonata in A Major, K331**, followed by his most wonderful **ADAGIO in b minor, K540**, a work greatly challenging in its depth and brilliance. The programme that afternoon was brought to a close with the marvellous **PIANO QUARTET in G Minor, K478**, which I performed with the Slovenian Trio. It was fun to note the obvious curiosity of the group as they wondered how this **String Trio**, who had just entered, would perform the programmed **Quartet**. More fun when I rose from my seat to join the other three! This beautiful piano quartet, (one of only two Mozart wrote) has been described as "a synthesis of chamber music and concerto ". It is certainly a most challenging work and I had managed only two (**secret**) rehearsals with the Trio at the Academy of Music. So it was a lovely surprise for them.

Our tour continued with an excursion to the island of BLED, the cruise to Venice (yes **THAT** year's one, earlier described!!) some time in Milan and Nice (doing all those things one does in both places), with Chris speaking about the wines of the region on a trip to see the seven beautiful gardens of the amazing belle époque Villa Ephrussi de Rothschild on a point at St Jean Cap Ferrat. Deborah gave an excellent talk about Henri Matisse at the special Museum named for him high above Nice. Then a visit to St Paul de Vence and finally, by plane and bus, to **BADEN-BADEN** in Germany...looked forward to as one of the highlights of this tour.

This lovely small city, situated among mountains and huge pine forests had for two centuries attracted the aristocracy (especially the Russians) and notably the great Russian writer, Ivan Turgenev. Dostoyevsky visited quite often to argue with Turgenev. Liszt, Rubenstein and others came and Clara Schumann bought a house here after the death of her husband, Robert, and was usually accompanied by her great friend, Johnnes Brahms, and others. Clara had had a long friendship with Pauline Viardot, who at one time, had been closely involved with Chopin, but who had for twenty years conducted a strange and highly complicated relationship with Turgenev.It was probably entirely innocent, she a married woman with children. But tongues were always wagging, and it is fun to think of all the intrigue and gossiping at the weekly music gatherings in her home in Baden-Baden, which Clara Schumann, Brahms, Liszt and so many more regularly attended. I have always adored the idea of these open weekly artistic gatherings...no set invitations. Those in the know, just knew where and when...and turned up! Wouldn't it have been superb? Why don't we still do this? The fashion petered out. All too expensive perhaps? A different world. But what a loss. Why don't we think further about this?

The most significant building in Baden-Baden is the superb Festspielhaus, which houses Germany's largest opera house and concert hall. This richly endowed house has become an extremely important venue on the international music circuit. It was here we heard the Berlin Philharmonic conducted by Sir Simon Rattle. What an experience; **Beethoven Fifth; Berlioz "Romeo and Juliet"**; and **Stravinsky "Agon"**.) There is another matter of great importance here...all young people under the age of twenty-five, have free entrance to all performances. This is an excellent way of encouraging a life-long knowledge and interest in the Arts.

Our stay in Baden-Baden was delightful. It has an air of quiet luxury but never ostentatious. Elegant. Beautifully served meals, a memorable excursion in the Black Forest and a visit to the Chagal Retrospective.

Onwards now for the famous **Alsace/Lorraine Wine route** commencing in beautiful Strasbourg. Chris gives a very informative talk about these marvellous wines and we stop in beautiful **RIQUWIHR** to visit the famous **Hugel Winery.** The Manager, David Ling, standing in for Etienne Hugel, remembers our Australian friends, Mavis and Jack Crittenden (Crittenden Wines) who had visited previously on another LINGUA MUSICA tour, and joins us for a delightful luncheon after some very enjoyable 'tastings', during which we bought a few bottles of his excellent pinot gris and traminers. Another stop en route was very pretty **RIBBEAUVILLE,** (which has an annual ancient music festival. Could just imagine it in such a setting). We did not go on to beautiful COLMAR (which I had previously included)...insufficient time. But finally our arrival in Burgundy, at the ancient **Chateau de Gilly,** now a 5 star hotel. Every one delighted and happy to relax after this long day. Chris tells us a lot about the various beautiful Burgundies and the history of the wine industry in this region, before a marvellous dinner in their fabulous cloistered restaurant. It is a great experience. Chris has also invited a French colleague, Gilles Duroche, to speak about his own cellars and his own particular grand crus. I have to say, I found this rather a waste of space as he was speaking only about said grand crus @ approximately Eur 250 a bottle (meaning over $ 500 a bottle in Australia) and I couldn't quite see the point. We were not about to buy such over-priced items, though I suppose it was interesting to hear about that side of the industry....for those in a financial category who could support it.

Next day, Chris led a visit to nearby **BEAUNE**... another small city full of historical interest even apart from all the wineries here and also the manufacture of ancient wine coopers. And in the evening our Farewell Dinner...again in the Chateau's restaurant. It is a really happy occasion and the wines are superb. Lovely speeches and they present me with a charming little gift. (An amusing little incident here, when Deborah notices her main course is still slightly frozen! We anxiously look around the table and thankfully see no signs elsewhere.)

The final day of this Wine section of the 2006 tour will be in **DIJON**, which we normally only associate with mustard. But it is so so much more than that....wines, markets, delightful architecture, interesting history,...and yes, 'la moutarde'! From here, one of those great TGV's will bring the group to Paris.

I think back to that breakfast at the Cope-Williams' almost a year before. Yes Kathie, it was a good suggestion!

"2007.....A TOUR WITH A DIFFERENCE"

It is interesting now to reflect on those expensive, time-consuming and tiring pre and après-tour research trips I used always to do. And always at break- neck speed, but in those early days, considered by me to be very necessary. In so many instances, I was returning to locations I had not visited for many years and needed to feel absolutely secure about all inclusions within locations...hotels booked, correct doors to use, correct directions to take, meal possibilities and costs...details of all kinds. Lately I have been amused when re-reading some of the hastily scribbled notes I used to make in my personal tour diaries. Some barely readable. Loose pages now missing. These words were intended for no one but myself of course. Suggestions, comparisons, foods, costs, descriptions of some difficult railway entrances and what to avoid. How I felt at different times, how to avoid unnecessary inclusions. All useful, all time-consuming. But after many years, I finally abandoned this extra effort. I was completely confident with all the inclusions and details of the cities I was including on the tours I offered. What I now did was to ensure that the first arrangement in each place was a guided tour with a local expert booked well ahead; and while this happened, I would swiftly check out anything I needed to check. And so it went...**till 2007.**

At a reception after a concert in Melbourne, I had been introduced to the wonderful violinist, **JULIAN RACHLIN**, who told me of the annual **"Julian Rachlin and Friends Festival"** he had been organising every year since 2001 in **DUBROVNIK**, and "Why don't you bring a group there for the next?" When in Slovenia, I had travelled a little further south into Northern Croatia, had heard so much about its beautiful Dubrovnik and other interesting places but had never been further south. So why not? Julian Rachlin (b. 1974) is considered one of the most exciting and respected musicians of our time. He plays the 1704 ex leibig Stradivari loaned him by a very important cultural foundation. And the UNESCO world heritage-listed little city of Dubrovnik was certainly a great temptation for me. So, why not? And I got to work, planning something new.

The trouble was that the year 2007 was also a very very busy personal one for me. I had to be in Toronto for the "Name Day" of Mia, my tiniest new granddaughter, which was a simply delightful and moving occasion. (Had also stopped off in New York for a few days en route and tiny Mia's other granny who lived there took me sightseeing and we spent a long time in that wonderful Metropolitan Museum, where I could happily spend days). And after Toronto, on to London, for the very earliest discussions with Terry Lewis and Ruth Nye, and various other meetings regarding the proposed new book I was to write. I had advertised this extended new tour months before and it was already well booked, but the unknown to me Dubrovnik/ Zagreb inclusions of this needed actually to be checked out...SOMEHOW. I set apart five days before group arrival and made it happen, so that afterwards I would have a couple of days to recover. It was full on, but actually an enjoyable experience on my own. I wandered, took notes, checked reservations and made further ones, observed, reflected, and relaxed. Thought it might be fun to include a little of my personal notes from that particular research trip, that is, if I can possibly unscramble my scribbles! We'll see.....

Arrival at Dubrovnik Airport easy...amazing to think just so recently had been occupied by an unfriendly army...a bit scary to consider actually.Thank heavens no signs of the terrible fires as we drive into the city. The tiny guest house, Musika,utterly charming and with small garden.. can you believe it washing line and pegs! Just relax. Pot of tea and guest biccies...too tired to go out to dinner. Just short walk. Early next morning, driver/guide, Tony, takes me into Old City...so beautiful. As expected, a walled one and shown evidence of the recent terrible fighting, bullet holes in the walls. Horrible to see this.

Sad. I wander alone...no stress...marvellous. Easy to find the Rector's Palace for the concerts, all restored and beautiful again... but need to check out restaurants and EXACT turns and timings to get there from the chosen hotel (EXCELSIOR)...damn, it's quite uphill, though they have insisted only 10 mins outside walls. Why didn't they describe more exactly? Anyway, over the top 5 star luxury and gorgeous terraces above sea from every room...amazing for the manageable price I have paid. So much better than further north. Love it. Arrange the Welcome Dinner on main terrace and they give me a welcome drink out there. It's already rather warm...but nice..will enjoy just sitting here short time.. 30 mins. Check watch. Incredible to see out on horizon one of those ghastly vulgar multi storey cruise ships. Why would they allow them here? Waiter (all speak English) says they all come into town on ship launch, wander around, spend nothing and then go back to have all meals and drinks on ship. Mostly Yanks and Japs. Goodness. Must make myself some strict notes...10 mns. back down hill...easier. Entrance gate to city, turn left, then right (should that have been left again?) into square...the street surfaces very shiny...the ancient marble newly restored...bit slippery actually if it rained I would have thought, and the recommended restaurant, LOCANDA, apparently well known. Get here, make group reservation, discuss menu, cannot believe the prices, sit here and have delicious fried sardines, salad and small glass of chilled white, 'Posip Smokvica' (it's suddenly very warm) right beside boats...gorgeous.....so relaxing. Work out this lunch is costing me about $15 plus the wine! Feel almost ashamed to be paying so little. Love it and enjoy very brief conversation with little family from Genoa next door..2 children with curls and sparkling dark eyes...turn back for my camera. My Camera... there on table two minutes ago, has gone!! Frantic. Manager comes...so concerned, tries to help...questions people...but of course...gone! How/ Who? So quickly? The wretches are so clever. But must remember to report to Police or no later claim possible.Where are they? Probably not inside walls.Can't be bothered now...but must later, on same day. Important same day. I go on.... left, 10 mins or so, and opp the Rector's Palace nice restaurant with pretty pink cloths outside. Make another group one there for after 2nd concert (TEATAR...pasta dishes kuna 55...salads about k 22...present Croatia exchange rate AUD 4.888, Eur 7.20.) Quite a variety of choices. Great....

they will just love it. Wait and collect concert tickets when bureau reopens... pre-paid from Oz. Like Spain, they close for ages in middle of day. So annoying. While I wait around I consider the horrifying things which happened during the Bosnian War...and yes, Dubrovnik, which had nothing to do with it, being under siege in 91/92. So terrible.Such damage. What a great spirit here. We know nothing of war in our country. These poor people....Getting tired...want to get back to my little house for a rest.Dinner this evening with Kesenija who will pick me up.. looking after arrangts. Plan the excursion to Montenegro.(Tony is NOT happy about this...splutters in disgust.) Of course the war is so recent and the Montenegro damage to cultural Dubrovnik horrifying....68% of the buildings damaged, including The Rector's Palace...all wonderfully restored now of course.. Better keep quiet about it...but they will want to see M. only 45 mins away and get a feel of those times. Pity not time to extend further...Sarejevo etc, but that is 240 kms away....can't do everything. Feel strangely guilty about this. Should have. Had heard so much from Volodja in Ljubljana about the way the Slovenians had extracted themselves from Yugoslavia in 1991...and feel I wanted to respect in some way the people who suffered the horrors of the entire Bosnian War. Hard to explain. Tony has gone silent. 5am next morning, Tony rings (have no alarm) and collects me for airport and 50 min flight to Zagreb. He has been such a help...lovely young man...they expect first baby. Will their lives here be ok? Do hope so. Don't know what to expect but taxi easy and hotel is lovely and opposite parklands. Again the costs manageable and have paid most well ahead. I need to get out to explore the capital....don't know it at all...larger than expected. Seems nice enough. Academy of Music close...the concert will be there. As planned meet the Australian Ambassador, Tracey Reid, OAM, who is charming. We have a great talk over coffee and she tells me about her life here and that her husband is her helper with the children. (So nice to hear this opposite situation). We don't speak of the War, though am tempted. She will join the group for cocktails at the arranged time...may, or may not bring her husband... depends on baby sitter.I am sure group will have plenty of questions for her....incl the war. Will that be permitted I wonder? Diplomatic reserve? Must get on with city walks (after late lunch under large awnings overlooking fountains)...little children playing in and out water...so lovely to see. Feel so nostalgic...and *suddenly very alone. Lonely. Stop it...get on. Pity it's all so steep....steps everywhere. My lungs don't like all this climbing. But discover so much from my printed guide, "Know Zagreb". Make notes. Just reading and trying to follow the maps...a bit confusing. Need to get back to hotel in time to do some practice in that large room with the piano. So maybe leave a lot till tomorrow? Speak with Banqueting Manager...all will be ok. Ring restaurant and simple dinner on a tray brought to my room....windows open to balcony and parks below. People riding bikes. Up not too early, coffee/croissant and off... must get to the cathedral...St Stephens (but also referred to as 'Assumption'...can't figure that out...dedicated to Our Lady of the Assumption perhaps?) Gregorian chant Mass in progress...utterly gorgeous interior, even delicate chandeliers... soft gentle colours...star studded ceiling...choir perfect and congregation joining where appropriate. Takes me back to primary school days and Gregorian Chant...amazing kids we must have been...10/11? yr olds? Able to remember all the Latin and follow that quite difficult medieval music notation in our Dr.Percy Jones hymnals? No special musical ability with most of that class, so how on earth? Oh yes, Mother Vincent....beautiful voice, very tall. beautiful face...those cheek bones..very commanding presence, but nice..always rewarding us...sweets, let out 5 mins early. Amazing really.yes....amazing. haven't thought about it in years. Oh dear...Here I am years later and other side of world.Goodness yes...amazing. Suddenly back in present.Here it is absolutely packed and am squashed in a side row and thinking such long ago things. A bit ridiculous. But feel so very moved by it all right now the present music and the memories, at times tears...embarrassing.... a few stares, but I don't care..no one knows me. Then tiny girl..3 maybe?.. with chubby hand on my knee stares into my face with that worried intensity....I smile...hope reassuringly...at her. It's ok...really. Young mother, embarrassed, gently removes her hand and averts her eyes. Lovely people. Kind. A stranger in their midst. And I think so much of my beloved family so far away. Later light candles for them all...a lot!!!! Must get a move on. In the Treasury below, many wonderful 11th and 12^{th}c exhibits...if only more time...but they will see it all with guide. Take details of restaurant opposite...KAPOLSKA...will make reservation here...closed now. Steep streets but funiculars too. great! See the famous 13^{th}c pharmacy, Parliament and the 20^{th}c sculptor's house...can't remember his* name but no matter. Famous St Catherine's. (why famous?) time to get back, but stop in another lovely lower square. Check again prices of various dishes.... yes, not imagining it...so affordable. Not cheap...affordable. Tired. Grab a taxi back to hotel (still trying to work out the connection between St Stephen's and Assumption. Must remember to ask.) Practise just one hour...memory ok. Piano not too bad. 6am call. Taxi to airport...flight delayed... don't care. Rest...nice flight and arrival Heathrow, long walk and the quick 15 min express to Paddo. Group will arrive in two days time. All is well at the fashionable Lancaster Hotel nearby....popped in to double check everything, make sure No smoking rooms. Guide fine, driver fine, Albert Hall tickets fine, theatre ones fine, Airport transport to Gatwick fine. Phew...Need a day or two for myself...hairdresser and manicure usual place round corner. Terry takes me to lovely afternoon recital by Angela Hewitt in Cadogan Hall (Bach, Scarlatti and others)as always, wonderful...notice her very high red heels!She is her usual delightful self afterwards. Snatch an hour to practise my own Scarlatti at JS Pianos and ring Ruth....yes will come down to farm after the tour. Have restful two nights, just slipping round corner for a bite at "ASK"... always so easy here alone....never awkward. Manager remembers me.... tired....

This tour commenced in **London, then Dubrovnik, Zagreb**, followed by **Ljubljana, Eisenstadt,** (Joseph Haydn's long connections with Royal Family here. Wonderful concert in the Castle...Esterhazy Hall. Marvellous experiences. But oh, need to emphasise, (usually considered trivial fact, but absolutely NOT!) Must always remember that if walking long distances on cobbled streets, STURDY shoe soles an absolute must. Had left mine in London this time and in light shoes did some damage here. Took weeks to recover! Hobbled around remainder of tour. There was the usual packed **Vienna** schedule (mostly Imperial Vienna) where Beethoven, Schubert, Brahms, Mahler, Freud, Klimt, Kockoshka, Kandinsky are only some of those notables who considered this city the only possible place to live and continue their work, a concert in the Goldener Saal of the famous Musikverein and also The Vienna Boys' Choir in the Palace Chapel (see note below). Then very steep picturesque UNESCO- listed **Chesky Crumlov**, such an incredibly pretty place, once annexed by the Nazis but after the 1989 Velvet Revolution, beautifully restored and absolutely gorgeous to visit. They all adored it.(I sat it out. Lovely rest!) Travelling in our private bus, there were one or two stops in less known but lovely places along the way. A similarly packed **Prague** several days. 'Don Giovanni' in the Estates Theatre where Mozart had actually premiered it in 1783, history around every corner, guided walks, and I recall so vividly our final dinner in a popular outside restaurant in the square after their final concert at the great Rudolfinum. They would not reserve the tables, so I gave up my concert ticket and tried to 'hold' two large round tables. Head waiter not having any of this. I had to pay ahead for a decided menu if I wanted to hold them. Thought about it briefly. This group had had to put up with a hobbling and not quite so energetic leader over past week, and I wanted the tour to finish on a celebratory note. Groaned inwardly and paid, knowing I would have to pay more again later. It was not that much actually. Had a glass of wine and managed to hold off for an hour and a half the angry protesters who wanted these places…quite a feat. But in the end, so worth it. They were all ecstatic about their concert and finishing outside in such a setting. We all flew back to London next morning, most of them onwards to Australia and a few heading off on a bus tour around England. So that was 2007. For me, a rather remarkable tour I think.

VIENNA BOYS' CHOIR:

An important part of Austria's musical life, this wonderful Boys' Choir has enchanted people around the world for more than five centuries. It dates back to 1498, and later the Habsburg monarchs encouraged and supported musical life in general and this Boys' Choir in particular. Some of Austria's most famous musicians received their training in the ranks of this then Imperial Choir. Today, when not touring, the choir sings the Mass every Sunday in the Chapel of the Hofburg Palace, Vienna.

Australia also has an important connection with this famous choir. When WW2 broke out, the choir on tour and then in Melbourne, was stranded. They were billeted with various families and one can only imagine the distress and loneliness of these little boys, despite every kindness and care given them. Their education continued as an Australian one, and after the war, many opted to remain in their new country, a few having their Austrian family eventually join them there, ie. if they had not lost their lives in Concentration Camps. Many became integrated into the Australian musical world, married, and later started their own Australian families in their adopted country.

I personally have a special reason to remember them. As a teenager, I was the organist in my local parish church where the choir master was the charming and oh so musical **STEFAN HAAG** (who some years later went on to become Director of Opera Australia). Stefan became a close family friend and my memories of wonderful musical evenings in our home around the piano with Stefan and occasionally others from the original choir are still very strong. I remember with a thrill, on one occasion he sang the Schubert "Earl King" once he discovered I could play it well enough to accompany him. It is a difficult work. I remember Stefan telling my parents that had they returned to Austria before being stranded here, they most probably would all have lost their lives. So for them, though tremendously difficult as little boys, they had gradually begun to realise how fortunate they had been. More importantly, when my husband and I married, Stefan Haag got together as many as possible of 'The Boys' (as he called them) to sing at Roma's wedding. So we had the great privilege of having THE VIENNA BOYS' CHOIR helping to celebrate our special day with a beautiful rendition of a Mass by Franz Abt (1819 -1885), a famous Austrian composer of that time. This is certainly a most treasured memory, and I have always wished it had been recorded. Alas not.

I have another small memory of Stefan Haag: He was a fabulous dancer. I can remember whenever he waltzed with me at the Parish dances, he used to take me, in great sweeps in a reverse direction around the floor from the other dancers! My teenage heart used to leap with joy as I was transported by those marvellous Viennese waltzes! Ah...youth!

"LISZT BICENTENARY AND MORE"

Franz Liszt: 1811-1886:

This very full and diverse 2011 tour did not totally concentrate on Franz Liszt, but its major focus was indeed the Bicentenary of his birth on October 22nd, 1811, at Raiding, 30 miles from Esterhazy (then Hungary) and really not very far from Vienna, the musical capital. He was of course an amazing child prodigy and his father decided they must move to Vienna for the musical education of his little son. The story goes that Beethoven heard the little boy, mounted the stage and kissed him. May or may not be true. But certainly his career took off in an extraordinary manner. Soon Paris and elsewhere. At this time, the amazing violinist, Paganini, was taking Europe by storm. Liszt decided to become the "Paganini of the Piano", and did he ever! He performed everywhere. It was Liszt, in fact, who more or less revolutionised public concerts. He actually invented what we came to know as the Solo Recital. He was glorified, he was mobbed, women fainted, everyone wanted him. But gradually he was tiring of all this display. He knew he had more serious concerns. Settling in culturally conscious Weimar, he began to study, to compose, to guide, to lead. He created a new major musical edifice in this cultural centre and gave lessons without fee to those with special talents and importantly to him, the right attitude. His personal life became more considered. The beautiful and cultured Marie d'Agoult became his partner and they fled to Geneva for a time. In Paris of course he had been friendly with Frederic Chopin whose music he greatly admired and who would claim that "No one performs my music better than Liszt", (but, strangely, without ever praising Liszt's own composition). But Liszt was increasingly questioning himself and his ambitions, and by the age of only 37 years, he cut himself off from public life and never returned. He donated all the money he had ever earned publicly to worthy causes and set himself to help others. It is perhaps a little surprising that at this time he also developed an association with the Polish Princess Carolyne von Sayn-Wittgenstein, who shared his intellectual views. They became very serious about a future together but she was not able to gain a divorce. Still, they did manage some limited life together, however difficult. Liszt greatly admired the work of Wagner (never quite realising how the latter used him) but was dismayed when his daughter, Cosima, left her marriage to the great conductor, von Bulow, and married Richard Wagner. Liszt increasingly moved inside himself, becoming deeply religious, and even taking initial holy orders at one stage. His final twenty years of composition were deeply reflective ones. One particularly turns to his three years of travel and musical thought, his wonderful "Annees de Pelerinage" collection, which opened up many new means of expression. Liszt spent his final years in deep contemplation at the beautiful Villa d'Este north of Rome.Greatly weakened in health, he travelled the then exceedingly difficult long distances to be with his son-in-law, daughter and grandchildren for the opening of Wagner's festival in Bayreuth. Unfortunately it was all too much for him and he died there. It is very moving to be in Bayreuth and to see evidence of this.

For a long time in Europe, the music of Franz Liszt was considered too exhibitionist...without depth. Not understood.The great Chilean maestro, Claudio Arrau, was one of the first to correct this view and to show the extraordinary depth and beauty of his compositions. His later star pupil, Ruth Nye, took up this challenge and has presented much of the later work of this genius in her recitals. Another Australian pianist and scholar, Leslie Howard, made it almost a life-time work to record and write about the entire output of Franz Liszt. Leslie Howard claimed that Liszt suffered mostly from the jealously of others.

So, this tour: We started off doing everything one does in **VIENNA,** (including a greatly remembered "La Traviata" with Natalia Dessay....so tiny but with such a BIG voice). Then, leaving most of our things there, took a fast train journey to **BUDAPEST** for three days, where of course, among all else in that beautiful city, we attended the Liszt Academy and Museum as well as a great performance of The Karamazovs (music by Rachmaninov and other Russians) at the Hungarian State Opera House. My assistant (this time, eldest granddaughter, Caroline, then having recently completed her degree in Paris and working in Rome) brought all our cases etc to meet us at Vienna Airport and we flew to **LEIPZIG.** Great concert at the Gewandhaus, great walks and tours, lunch in the cafe where Bach had lunched, the wonderfully restored Bosehaus, Auerbach's Keller, and of course, a simply wonderful musical service in the renowned St Thomas Church of J.S.Bach fame. As mentioned earlier in this work, Johann Sebastian Bach (1685 – 1750) the absolute master, who brought the contrapuntal style of composition to its very peak, lived and worked in Leipzig. As organist and director at St.Thomas Church, he was charged with providing a new cantata for each week of the year. How he managed to do all he did, as well as teach and care for his very large family is almost beyond comprehension. Here also, I gave a recital in the music room of the charming Mendelsshon Home. (Very moving to see the tiny study and desk where he composed. I understand he always did so, standing up).Travelling a little later in the year than usual, the sun shone, the air was crisp and invigorating and the beautiful Autumn colours were already well advanced. October is actually a wonderful time to be in Europe.

Travelling on in our bus to nearby **WEIMAR,** we were all looking forward to October 22nd, where the actual principal celebration of Liszt's Bicentenary was to happen at the newly opened extravagant **WEIMAR CONCERT HALL.** It was indeed a great event. Staying in the famous Elephant Hotel, Ruth Nye, who had just arrived, gave an excellent lecture and also, visiting French pianist, Emmanuel Despax, a wonderful Liszt recital (including his huge **Dante Sonata**,) and we all visited the charming home on the edge of the lovely surrounding woods in which Liszt had once lived. The obvious simplicity of his life then was extremely moving. Liszt, the great master living so simply and inexpensively.! Then we joined the beautifully dressed international audience for the provided pre-concert champagne and canapés, followed by several welcoming speeches, and finally, finally, this 200th birthday concert. The orchestra conducted by Christian Thielemann, presented a most exacting programme. **Wagner: 'Overture to Tannhauser'; Liszt: Piano Concerto No 2 in A major**; and **Liszt: Tottentanz**. The Russian soloist, Konstantin Scherberkov was impressive. It was a marvellous celebration and we walked back to The Elephant in an exuberant mood. (I recall Ruth, Terry and a few of us close friends sitting up and enjoying a very late private party with some very amusing conversations we still laugh about today!).

During the Weimar days, we did a full day trip to **BAYREUTH**. Such a pretty little city and the one chosen by the extraordinary composer, writer and political agitater, Richard Wagner, for the location of his Festival Opera Haus as a venue in which to promote (among other things) his strange ideas about the future of Germany. He founded a Wagner Festival here which still brings Wagner enthusiasts, especially to hear his 'Ring Cycle'. It is a beautiful place. (I am not particularly fond of Wagner's music, especially 'The Ring'. But I can remember vividly how as a seventeen year old university student, hearing his 'Siegfried Idyll' at an Aesthetics lecture and thinking it the most beautiful music I had ever heard). Wagner and family (despite their borderline poverty) lived truly sumptuously, thanks to his royal supporter, King Ludwig (often referred to as 'Mad King Ludwig '...he was certainly rather undisciplined in his behaviour and his views at times.) Wagner's Bayreuth (quite apart from the general Bayreuth) is also a place with some extraordinary ideas about humankind. The Festival is dutifully maintained by his successors, but there have been one or two later Wagners who have questioned the original ideas which had been promoted here. Needless to say, not exactly popular with those fighting to retain the mystique and what, frankly, is the 'family business'. But for all that, it's a beautiful place, where emphasis on physical fitness (walking, skiing, tennis etc) means we see suntanned healthy sporty people everywhere. They are also charming and welcoming. I have a special friend in Bayreuth who lives in a most delightful historic apartment and who has entertained my tour guests here on every visit to her city. She has her own ideas regarding the Wagners, but wisely keeps them to herself. The house where Franz Liszt died is one we always visit.

The tour continued to **VENICE** and thence an hour north to the gorgeous little village of **SACILE** where is the headquarters of FAZIOLI PIANOS. It is a very pleasant building, not at all like a factory...very quiet, with the technicians bent intently over their specific tasks. The only sound to break this silence is the occasional gentle musical one. Sacile is where the local pianist and absolute genius, Paulo Fazioli, realised that the spruce from the straight tall trees growing in the nearby forest would be perfect for the soundboards of a new piano. Now so many great international concert pianists have gone from Steinway to Fazioli. My dear friend, Terence Lewis, is the General Manager of Jacques Samuel Pianos in London, which is also the British Fazioli headquarters. Terry gave a wonderful demonstration of the hand crafting of these amazing instruments. There is not one detail of this creation about which he is unfamiliar. The tour members were fascinated and part of the attraction was the fact that Terry is a fine pianist himself and has such an engaging and delightful manner.

Afterwards we enjoyed a beautiful recital in the Fazioli Hall given by a young Italian pianist, David Malusa and finished the evening with a wondrous banquet (the only possible word for this event). Our guests of honour are Ruth Nye and the maestro himself...Paulo Fazioli.

The very fast express down to **ROME** is a welcome experience with lunch en route and settling into a wonderful hotel right on the Walls, which had been host over the years to so many international musicians was easily managed. Naturally a well designed program had been arranged for Rome....all the usual visitations in the Eternal City, some of it conducted by Caroline who had already lived and worked in Rome for a couple of years.(Our Caroline is truly a linguist. At that stage, fluent French, Italian and Spanish, and since then, several more languages). I am always amazed by people with such linguistic skills.

A most important remembrance from this time was a visit a little north to the beautiful Villa d'Este, where Liszt had spent his final years. After an exploration of those wonderful gardens and waterfalls (the subject of Liszt's "Fountains of the Villa d'Este "which Ruth Nye has recorded so brilliantly), a lovely lunch in Tivoli, and then Ruth gave a most wonderful and moving recital of late Liszt works. That was a magical time. Ruth's recital from that Villa d'Este visit is now, with so many other works she plays, able to be heard on U Tube. Ruth Nye and Terry Lewis left us here for their flights back to London.

The rest of us returned to Rome. A wonderful performance of the ballet, 'La Bayadere' (a second time for this particular ballet on a LINGUA MUSICA tour) in the Teatro del Opera di Roma, a visit to The Vatican, a coffee stop and discovery walk in Strastevere (that delightful 'village' within the city); and this tour concluded with a happy Farewell Dinner in the restaurant of our beautiful Hotel Victoria Roma.

The 2011 Liszt Bicentenial Tour was a truly successful one in every way. An excellent well matched group and every arrangement fell into place so well, plus having such wonderful musicians travelling with us. It is a very satisfying and thankful feeling for me to have after a tour such as this.

FURTHER MOMENTS RECALLED

MUSIC PERORMANCES:

Well, looking back over thirty years of tours, I loosely estimate the following enjoyed by my tour groups:
OPERA and BALLET: probably **at least** 120 opera performances
SYMPHONY AND CONCERTO: At least 100 performances
SOLO RECITALS: At least 160 performances.

Some great names and music venues emerge from a recent perusal of the Tour Handbooks...just a few of those our groups experienced, no particular order or category:

Isaac Stern, Beaux Arts Trio, Mauzio Pollini, Simon Rattle, Claudio Abbado, Yehudi Menuhin, Rostropovitch, Concertgabou, Richard Markson, Ruth Nye, Emmanuel Despax, Oberammagau Passion Play, Vienna Staatsoper. Amael Chamber Trio, Lorin Maazel, John Eliot Gardiner, Berlin Symphony Orchestra, Vienna Symphony Orchestra, London Symphony Orchestra, Albert hall, Emma Kirkby, Hannu Lintu, Alicia de Larocha, Pieter Wispelwey, Zubin Mehta, Chopin Manor, Rektor's Palace, Mariss Janson, Gewandhaus Leipzig, Mendelssohn Conservatory, Angela Hewitt, Trasimeno Festivals, Duszniki Dzroj Chopin Festivals, Felicity Lott, Jeffrey Tate, Christian Thielman, Leslie Howard...I could go on and on, there are many more I could add...but you will be pleased, that I shall not! And yes, this veritable alchemy of music venues and great performers...every single one of the above was most certainly experienced on the L/M tours.

(Oct 14th: Listening to a simply beautiful recording of Jacqueline du Pres

playing the Haydn cello Concerto No 2 with the LSO on our wonderful Classic FM with Martin Buzacott. Incredible legato...seemed no physical involvement at all. How well I remember seeing this passionate young musician performing when we lived in London in the swinging sixties. It saddens me now that I could not have added her name to the above list. Her terrible disease caused her to stop playing in 1973 and she died, so young.)

THEATRE: Some six that I can remember.

GALLERIES: Always, guided visits by art experts to the most famous museums and galleries in Europe.....too many to remember them all. Perhaps the most significant being the three greats in Madrid, but so many others, always the most famous in every location.

GUEST LECTURES: I think there would have been about 50 such....quite apart from the on- tour lectures from Clive Stark, myself, Deborah and Jackie on works, composes, art and other topics.

GUIDED EXCURSIONS: Innumerable...by train, coach, water, to some of the most memorable and exquisite regions of Europe....even an overnight one by ship.

PERSONALITIES: As I have already written, meeting some of the most distinguished musical personalities performing at diverse locations during these many years on tour. Almost always, artists at the very top of their fields, were kind enough to speak with my groups.

DIPLOMATIC MEETINGS: The Australian Ambassador in Paris, His Excellency, John Spender, loaned his private residence for a lecture recital by Ruth Nye. Australian Ambassadors or Consuls in various countries joined our groups for concerts and lunches etc. In Warsaw, His Excellency, Mr Patrick Lawless,(Australian Ambassador for Poland and Chzech Republic) invited the entire group to tea at his private residence.

This was a delightful occasion, children running by the pool, everything set out beautifully, and he and his wife mixing interestedly with the members of that large group. I recall he was especially interested to meet one tour member, whose father in law, Sir Rupert Clark, whom he knew well, had recently died. I sent the usual letter of thanks, hand-delivered by a porter at our hotel, and was very surprised and charmed immediately to receive one back from him, telling me what a delight it had been to have been able to enjoy conversations with such a culturally interesting group from his own country. Such things, he said, very rarely happened.

SOME FURTHER TOUR LOCATIONS :

BERLIN: Goodness, have I forgotten so far to mention several visits to Berlin? I do remember the first time I included this marvellous city on a tour outline. It was the first location on that tour. A couple who had already come with me twice asked if they could join at the next city... "We don't want to be in that sad and terrible place". Obviously the city had connotations with the war and the Nazis. Food for thought, and I admit to feeling a little anxious myself before that first arrival at the first location of that particular year's tour. I need not have been. Berlin is welcoming. It is beautiful. It is amazing. It is a city of parks...seemingly endless parkland. Beautiful avenues like the "Unter den Linden", a most interesting island of incredible art galleries and historical references, the lovely River Spree, and a city whose architecture mainly is the result of great international competitions. A city rebuilt after its almost total destruction at the end of the war. A city where one is forced to remember so many terrible facts and embrace with gratitude the end results of a nation's determination to regain the respect of the world and the ways in which they succeeded in doing so.

The Berlin Philharmonie of course was always very important on our visits to this great city. One of the most unconventional buildings in Berlin, it was designed by architect, Hans Scharoun, and completed in 1963. The Chamber Music Hall, by Edgar Wisniewski, was added in 1987. The Philharmonie Berlin is the home of the Berlin Symphony Orchestra. A renowned architect at the time of our first visit had written enthusiastically, "**Architecture as a Musical Instrument**: The three interlinked pentagons represent a move away from the infinite regularity of a square foundation to the most human of all symbols, the pentagon, as an age old symbol of life....the perfect harmonisation of man, music and space". Well, that's what he wrote, and Berliners and concert goers from everywhere seemed so excited about this new great edifice. Have to admit, though we experienced some superb concerts in that amazing hall, I was never really comfortable in such an interior. There are so many modern and "way out" concert halls around Europe which we visited. But I prefer the long established and secure acoustic of the traditional "shoe-box" concert hall design. An excellent example is The Goldener Saal of the great Musikverein in Vienna. But that is only one of so many such around the world, and in Australia. Very involved international investigations into the subject of Acoustics have concluded that the old, stable "shoe box" design is the most reliable for the production of a pleasing and satisfactory Acoustic for both listeners and performers.naturally, even within this design, there are many modern acoustical devices now... so often installed in the walls. Acoustic Engineers are extraordinarily inventive.

The **Berlin Philharmonic Orchestra** was founded in 1882 and remains one of the world's greats. Peter Tchaikowsky described it as having a unique quality, an "elasticity". He meant that they could very successfully adapt their playing to the music of any period. I find myself a little puzzled by this. Surely all great orchestras must need this so called "elasticity"? Undoubtedly though, some more than others. One of its most noted conductors was **Herbert von Karajan,** who died in 1989. **Claudio Abbado** succeeded him, and later, **Simon Rattle** (Sir Simon), who now is Chief Conductor of the London Symphony Orchestra, whilst guest conducting all over.

The Staatsoper Unter den Linden: Another great musical venue for us, has one of the richest operatic traditions in Germany. It was originally commissioned by Frederick the Great in 1740, and from its very earliest days, has been a magnet not only for opera lovers but for the world's greatest composers and musicians to this lovely site along that lovely boulevard....the Unter de Linden, with it beautiful trees. The orchestra of this great house, The Staatskapelle Berlin, has a tradition dating back more than 450 years.

Berlin's unique UNESCO listed **Museum Island** contains the following wonderful exhibition centres. The Alte and the Neue Museums, (we visited both), the Bode, the Pergamon and the Alte Nationalgalerie. Of all these, I do think the Pergamon was the one which left the most lasting impression on my groups, and most certainly on me. And in the Neues Museum... I close my eyes and immediately see the bust of Nefertiti, one of the most perfect sculptures to be seen anywhere. (My favourite visual art form is Sculpture and favourite Sculptor, Auguste Rodin, whose great works may be seen at the Musée Rodin in Paris.) But this Nefertiti, by the ancient Egyptian, Thutmose, in 1345 BC, now painted and stucco-coated in limestone, and since argued over for years between Germany and Egypt, is truly wonderful too.It is said these days to be a representation of 'modern woman' and a rival to Tutankhanum, which was found by the British, who at the time ruled Egypt. There is the extraordinary story of the British archaeologist, Howard Carter, finally chiselling his way into the tomb of this young pharaoh in 1922. He died soon after and according to mythology, anyone who penetrated this sacred tomb would die. All found to be such rubbish later on. But reading it did at the time, give me the shivers. Oh so so much could have been learned on these tours, if ONLY the time! One actually needs to **live** in European cities for at least some months before even the smallest degree of ancient histories can be properly known. Time....always Time... my greatest enemy.

Berlin abounds in wonderful parklands, the most accessible being The Tiergarten, in which one finds the famous Zoological Gardens from 1840, The Kurfurstendamn (known as theKu'damn) is its very busy main thoroughfare and starts from the deliberately still ruined and sad Kaiser Wilhelm Memorial Church to remind us of the destruction of this city in WW2 and its advances since that terrible time. Since the Wall separating East from West came down in 1989, the city also abounds with so many great hotels, restaurants, cafes and general life. Today (or rather, on our first visit) it's hard to imagine such senseless division. The new Reichstag, originally the site of the Parliament and which was set aflame and became a Nazi symbol, is a magnificent and quite awe inspiring building to visit, with its history in pictorial form along the curving ramp leading up to the top level, under the amazing new glass dome done by British architect, Sir Norman Foster. The Jewish Museum not far away is a completely different experience. Challottenburg Palace was another gorgeous place we enjoyed, and too much else to describe here.

So many lakes and woods surround Berlin, and a beautiful trip by water from Wannsee took us several times to nearby **Potsdam** and the simply beautiful Celelienhof Palace, where the felt overshoes are a must, and with its extensive and unique terraced gardens.It was actually here that Roosevelt, Churchill and Stalin met in 1945 to sign the so important Agreement at the end of WW2. Visit Berlin! And you will surely agree well worth it.

Young people seem to be very much attracted to Berlin.There is a healthy vibe and till the terrible pandemic, always much work experience available. But more recently, I have noticed the rise of an off-putting "far right" element in some of the young…gangs. In fact, on one occasion, standing alone on a train platform, I was bothered by such a group, both sexes, plus very intimidating dogs. I felt quite anxious. They were very aggressive, but actually of no consequence. The moment the Station Master appeared, they miraculously just seemed to evaporate…dogs and all. One minute they were there, the next gone. That apart, I do think Berlin is a great city to visit….so much of very great value to experience and learn.

Another city I should mention is **CORK**, in Southern Ireland. In 2005, quite surprisingly I felt, CORK was chosen by the European Community as that year's "Cultural Capital". (There was one such chosen every year, and often figured in my tours). Enormous work had been going on I understood all through 2004 and early in 2005, to improve the city in every possible way for this Cultural Capital festival period. I decided to include Cork and Dublin in that year's tour, called **"Music, Mountains and More "**.(I did mention at the beginning of my reflections regarding the setting up of the tours, that it was always such fun thinking up titles for each!) Inclusions that year were Copenhagen, Oslo, Bergen, Dublin, Cork, London and Vienna.

Cork is Ireland's second city and the capital of Munster. There was a quite extensive program in Cork, but the outstanding ones for me were a performance of the Monteverdi Vespers in Cork Cathedral by a distinguished Belgian group and another concert featuring the great soprano **EMMA KIRKBY** which I will never forget.It also took place in the cathedral, and her glorious voice soared in that lofty space. Born in Cambridge, Emma Kirkby studied Classics at Oxford whilst also having vocal training, though she never envisaged a musical career. She sang for pleasure but soon began to be 'noticed'. The world can be very grateful for this. Her range of recordings is impressive, from sequences of Hildegarde of Bingen, madrigals of the Italian and English Renaissance, cantatas, oratorios, operatic arias, Bach, Mozart and Handel. She sings it all. We adored her recital. Unfortunately, somehow or other, her printed program for that day is no longer among my papers, but I remember Bach, Handel and Telemann. Mostly I remember the voice! And it subsequently led me to seek out her recordings.

Another wonderful memory on that visit was a beautiful manor house not far from Cork City. **FOTA HOUSE** in Carraigtwohill (what a gorgeous place name!) for part of their Early Music Festival. Elegant yet homely, and set in beautiful grounds, it's library was the perfect setting for a performance of some breathtaking compositions of Marin Marais and St Colombe. Two wonderful Viola da Gamba players, Sarah Cunningham and Sarah Groser, were truly wonderful musicians in every way, with such a sense of balance, space, and yet directness. Marais, Couperin and St. Colombe. Marais's 'Tombeau de St. Colombe' was absolutely heartbreaking. Reduced a couple of us to tears. We don't hear enough of Marin Marais. There was a memorable Marais recital at the Conservatorium in Melbourne several years previously and thankfully I had bought some of his cd's. I enjoyed playing them again after this extremely moving event here at deliciously named "Carraigywohill" and its beautiful FOTA HOUSE. A memorable and thoughtful evening.

There were some guided tours and an excursion to pretty countryside which reminded me of Cornwall as well as afternoon tea for the whole group in the home of my very old friends, Nan and Dick Buckley, in delightful **KINSALE**, about an hour south of Cork, and often referred to as the 'Gourmet County Capital'. Naturally, we all adjourned for a super dinner down by the port afterwards So that was Cork! And next morning we flew off to London.

ANGELA HEWITT AND THE TRASIMENO FESTIVALS

Born into a Canadian musical family, Angela Hewitt began piano studies aged three, performing in public aged four and winning her first scholarship a year later. She lined and studied in Paris for several years. One of the world's leading pianists, Angela Hewitt performs solo as well as appearing with major orchestras all over the world...and several times in Australia. The Sunday Times in London has hailed her as "the pre-eminent Bach player of our time". The Guardian declared that "Angela Hewitt will define Bach performance on the piano for years to come". Of course this great pianist does perform and record the works of so many other composers, but perhaps it is Bach with whom we most associate her. She has taken on the enormous task to perform the entire works of Bach all around the world...her Bach Odyssey. She was made an Officer of the Order of Canada in 2000 and awarded an OBE in 2006. She lives in London and has also built a home on the edge of Lake Trasimeno in Umbria, Italy.

I got to know Angela during her visits to Melbourne, and also in London. She told me all about the annual festivals she had created in beautiful Umbria (which I actually enjoy more than Tuscany), and it was not long before I included a Trasimeno Festival few days as part of one of my annual tours. This was a great decision and was a truly magical experience and one we repeated three times, and planned to do so again in 2018, but Fate decided otherwise and I ended up having major surgery instead. Unhappily, like so many others in the artistic world today, Angela is holed up in isolation and the 2020 festival needed to be cancelled, but we hope 2001 will see her welcoming all her musical friends and supporters back to Perugia, Magione and all the villages surrounding the lake. If not 2021, then surely 2022.

Angela and her committee organise the entire week of high class performances in beautiful venues in this region of Umbria. She performs a lot herself, as well as inviting leading international artists. We have experienced superb performances in the great Cathedral of Assisi, in Perugia, in halls and theatres of several smaller towns/walled villages, and most fascinating of all, in the courtyard of the 11th century Castello di Magione. When she was discussing plans for her Italian house, Angela was taken to see this amazing medieval castle, fell in love with it, and immediately saw the wonderful roomy courtyard here as the perfect setting for a mid-summer music festival. The first such festival she created happened in 2004.

This ancient site had been owned by the Knights of Malta who had included small guest rooms for pilgrim travellers. After a very mixed history, it was acquired in 1979 by Count Marcello Cristofani, who donated it to the local magistrates. Then restoration commenced. Today, it is a fascinating example of what can be done by careful and historically mindful such restoration. The stunning inner courtyard, surrounded by its ancient stone balconies, is absolutely perfect for music performances on still summer evenings. Just occasionally there have been some hasty removals of Angela's Fazioli concert grand plus performers and attendees to a nearby venue when rain dampened the atmosphere...never the spirits. (A perfect example of the necessity of a reliable 'Plan B'!) We never experienced this...we were so fortunate that all visits to the Trasimeno Festival performances happened on gorgeous balmy evenings.

I can remember some magnificent concerts, one such being Angela performing with the Salzburg Academia in the magnificent Assisi Cathedral, another in the great Perugia Cathedral and so many more... especially in Magione. There were stays in delightfully located inns, great guided excursions through beautiful hilly countryside to charming elevated walled villages such as pretty flower filled Spello and so many,

many similar. Spello was very special, and had a particular personal remembrance for me of a short stay many years ago with my husband. There was another occasion about which I have a particularly amusing memory. I had arranged a pre-concert dinner in the courtyard of a most beautiful ancient hostelery in Trevi. We arrived to see the white clothed round tables set up and one long rectangular one for twenty in the centre. Seated at the very end of this table were two guys with their glasses of wine in earnest conversation. I realised there had been a little mix up and the waiter spoke briefly to the men who of course moved immediately to another table with many laughs and apologies. As they did so, one of my gorgeous group members asked one of these chaps, "Are you going to the concert after dinner too?" For a moment, he looked a little uncomfortable but then shrugged. "Actually I'm the conductor ". I felt I needed to intervene. It was the brilliant Hannu Lintu. "So sorry, maestro. Actually, I attended a concert you conducted in Melbourne a year or so ago". But he thought it all a great joke and said that Angela had mentioned an Australian group would be coming this evening. Angela laughed when told this story as she spoke with my group and moved around greeting many people before dinner was served. Afterwards we all walked through the winding small streets to a memorable concert in the ancient village theatre, in which of course, Angela joined the orchestra conducted by Hannu Lintu. The night was very warm and it was very pleasant afterwards to mix with members of an audience from all over the world in the pretty square outside the theatre. Another little non-musical memory I have from this evening...a thoughtful gesture by my eldest grandchild, Caroline, (Tour Assistant that year) who, unasked, suddenly whizzed into a tiny shop still open late and bought twenty bottles of water to hand out as we boarded our private bus back to our hotel located some distance away. Now that was a clever and most thoughtful gesture if ever there was one. It had been a very warm and thirsty evening! Most appreciated. Caroline, totally fluent in Italian, sat beside the young driver and they chatted animatedly the entire way. This girl speaks several languages. Linguists always amaze me.

So many utterly joyous experiences at several Trasimeno Festivals.

The foreign press has described it as being one of the most prestigious in Europe. I certainly agree and hope with all my heart that when this wretched world pandemic passes, we will again manage to experience the loveliness of this region and the glorious music in magical locations which Angela Hewitt and her dedicated team led by the local enthusiastic Maria Beneduce, organise for us all.

"TWO FESTIVALS TOUR"

In 1914 we did another really wonderful tour, combing the annual **BACH FESTIVAL** in Leipzig, Germany, and **THE TRASIMENO FESTIVAL** in Umbria, Italy. This included wonderful performances in the famous St.Thomas Church and St. Nikolai Church, both of J.S. Bach fame, as well as all the usual highlights of Leipzig, as mentioned earlier. We continued on to beautiful **WEIMAR**, with some great presentations there, including a visit to Liszt's later in life summer house, places associated with Goethe, and an excellent Lieder recital in Liszt's earlier grand place of residence, The Altenburg Palace. From here, some of our group took the option to visit nearby Buchenwald. It was a sobering experience for them. I did not go, having visited that sad place many years previously. We travelled on to beautiful **BAYREUTH** where we lunched in one of the most charming summer settings one could imagine, before our guide led the group on a very interesting walk tour, which included the famous Wagner Festival Theatre (used, at enormous expense, for such a short season each year) and his opulent residence, Wahfried...though actually not possible to enter this time, as it was undergoing extensive renovation. The small house where Liszt died was definitely included and my dear friend, who is a resident of Bayreuth, as usual, had us all to tea in her lovely historic apartment.

We continued on to **DRESDEN**, which is always a place of enormous interest and actually, quite an emotional experience. As is well known, it had suffered a veritable firestorm by the Allies during WW2, something which has been the subject of much discussion and criticism during the years since. The rebuilding of Dresden's most famous buildings is a story to fill a book...especially that of the beautiful Frauenkirche, which was painstakingly restored by the locals, brick by numbered brick, till its former magnificence was again there for us all to enjoy. It is the most inspiring story of total dedication. Of course the music performance at the great Semper Oper and the famous Zwinger Museum figured in this memorable stay.

From Dresden, we sailed down the beautiful River Elbe (a very welcome, relaxing trip) to **PRAGUE**, and all of those inclusions I have described earlier. Delightful little **CESKY KRUMLOV** (which everone adored) followed Prague and soon we were at the famous Hotel Bristol in **SALZBURG**, and all those wonderful experiences in this city that (incredibly) still claims Mozart. A superb concert in the Mirabell Palace and wonderful excursions to the magical **Salzkammergut**... Wolfgansee etc., where that special ice blue/green water of the lakes is so captivating. After lunch in the famous White Horse Inn, and further beautiful wandering, we fly off to Rome, and from there, in our coach to **PERUGIA**, for the Second Festival of this tour...Angela Hewitt's famous **TRASIMENO FESTIVAL**, commencing in the great cathedral of St Francis, Assisi, and continuing in gorgeous elevated Umbrian villages and the principal location of her festival...the famous Castello Magione. All the concerts organised by Angela and her committee, and in many of which she performs herself, were absolutely wonderful and it is here we have our Farewell Dinner and say goodbye for another year.

COPENHAGEN: There were two truly great visits here. It is such a lovely city in every way. A guided tour in the Footsteps of Hans Christian Andersen, charming canal tours (the perfect way to see Copenhagen), the Tivoli Gardens and the many summer performances always going on there, the lengthy, lovely Strogget shopping and gallery mall, river banks full of small cafes...and most important of all, the **HAMLET TOUR,** a full day one to ELSINORE and a performance of the Shakespeare play. Everyone was given a synopsis of this, arguably, the greatest of the master's works, after an excellent talk by the accompanying literary expert.

There were very good chamber music concerts in a beautiful church along the Strogget, and importantly, on one, a couple of water taxis across to the brand new **DR Koncerthustet**, designed by the French architect, Jean Nouvel. I can remember, as we approached, the deep cobalt blue of its exterior almost merging with the blue of the sky. This great complex actually contains four concert halls and the acoustic engineer for the principal one has been applauded world-wide for her success here, the manner in which the acoustic can be adjusted to each type of performance is a very impressive achievement. There are some beautiful squares in Copenhagen, and of course, everyone always hopes to catch a glimpse o "Our Princess Mary" and family cycling, as they so often do. But alas no. They did see their beautiful palace though, the Amelienborg Palace, actually one of four, on that beautiful square in Copenhagen. Crown Princess Mary has been an amazing success with the Danes. She has worked so hard and so loyally to win their love and respect. It is truly something of a fairy story. And quickly becoming fluent in that difficult language has always amazed me.

AMSTERDAM: Not sure if I have mentioned Amsterdam before. Yes I did....I mentioned it in relation to a very special concert at the famed Concertgabou, when we heard the music legend, the great violinist ISAAC STERN.The Concertgabou Orchestra is one of the most famous in the world and always a great privilege and delight for us to attend a concert there. I think we went to Amsterdam three times. The OLD CITY of Amsterdam is actually one of the largest city centres in the world. Capital of The Netherlands, the city is steeped in history, manifested in large and small buildings, 16th, 17th and 18th centuries, merchants' houses, museums etc along the famous canals of this beautiful and very lively city. It is a rich city, a very thriving city and respect for culture is very high. The major feature of the city is the Canal, where it is staggering to know that the beautiful houses lining its length were built on poles driven so far down under the surface of the water. It is often quite difficult to grasp this fact, because though looking solid and secure, they seem to float. The main problem in Amsterdam is that it is so crowded. But the people have solved this to a certain extent by riding bikes everywhere and of course, using the canals. This city prides itself on the richness of its Art and Music...the great **CONCERGABOU** for example, and the other concert venues. Van Gogh and Rembrandt are the BIG names here in the very famous **RIJKSMUSEUM**....but of course there are just so many more. We have done it all...lovely small squares often quite hidden and full of bookshops and cafes, lovely parks included, lovely walks and beautiful concerts and fantastic discoveries of great Art in both the Rijksmuseum and the Van Gogh one. The Hotel Marriot has been my favourite hotel in this unique city because of its location, allowing easy walking everywhere. Amsterdam's Schiphol Airport is considered to be the busiest in Europe (and oh how well I remember one tour member who discovered on arrival at our hotel that she had left her luggage there and had to be sent the 9 kms back in a taxi to retrieve it!) Perhaps not so well known is that there is a **Thaly's** train from here to Paris, which is a beautiful and very elegant and comfortable service we have enjoyed a couple of times. Thaly's is renouned for its first class habit of bring a beautifully served lunch on a tray to their passengers...complete with tiny flower arrangement and heavy linen napkins. If available, I would always travel Thaly's!

A few other tour memories...one associated with my friends, Meryl and Barry Axtens: I think it may have been 1993, and we had been in Venice. I had arranged a private bus transport from Venice to VERONA. A very nice trip till the bus breaks down! We are all standing around for an hour as the driver does his best and finally finds a solution. The Verona guide is waiting and charmingly understanding. While she takes the group on a guided tour, I have a coffee and wander alone, thinking what a really charming town Verona-without -the -crowds is. Meet them all at the famous Juliet House. We enjoy a delicious lunch before travelling on in a hastily changed van with our same driver, for SIENA. Here we are met by the Axtens. A nice evening's dinner and a small hotel after some walking in the famous central area associated with the equally famous horse race and the wonderful cathedral plus some discussion of plans for the next two days. Meryl has arranged some routes and visitations to places like charming Greve and also a wine tour. Must say, I enjoy the tastings and conversations in such vineyards, but after two hours of being shown the wine-making process, seemingly always the same, no matter where the vineyard and in which country, I tend to become a little disenchanted by it all). We enjoyed a couple of delightful Tuscan lunch stops in pretty and well known locations (including Greve), a delightful concert, and on the final night, Meryl and Barry had the entire group to dinner in their own house at Monterinaldi. She had made ahead the best and largest Tiramasu I had ever tasted! It was a great evening.

The following year, Meryl and Barry had arranged for my group a stay in the middle of our tour (they were not involved on the rest of this) in beautiful **Domaine de la Coste**. This beautiful property is situated in the Dordogne quite close to Sarlat and Domme, very favourite places for me and my husband. He was of course not with us, but my memories of our times there together were still clear. There was one couple on the tour that year who were sometimes quite difficult. This property consisted of several buildings (all charming in their own way) and accommodation had to be shared between this large group. The so called "Maison Principale" could not accommodate everyone. This had not been revealed to me beforehand or I would never have agreed to this stay. Naturally, decisions had to be made. Everyone seemed very happy with the allocations, except, of course, the trouble-makers, who complained about the inadequacy of their accommodation compared to others. A small committee had to "investigate"and declared the objections to be a nonsense. Still complaints, so another delightful pair offered to swap, and finally all was well. The main house had a beautiful large salon opening off the long dining room. In this was a grand piano and the Meryl had found and arranged an in- house concert by a local trio. It was a charming and successful evening. We did several visits to beautiful towns of the Dordogne from here. It was conveniently placed to do so. The Axtens did not stay with us. They left each evening for their own house not far away. (They then owned several houses in France which they let when the Brits all wanted to holiday in the Dordogne and elsewhere!!)

TOULOUSE: Another city which was included in two tours was Toulouse, in the south of France, often referred to as **THE PINK CITY**. This is because so many of the buildings in the Old city are of rose coloured stone and they glow as the sun sets or in certain lights. Toulouse is also noted as being the third largest university city in France. It is here that the annual **Printemps de Septembre Festival** as well as the **Jacobin Festival de Piano** take place. The concerts are given in the most beautiful churches and squares of the Old City with all its colour, and attract huge crowds to listen to the most distinguished performers in Europe. We managed to be there on two occasions when I recall that among the artists were Martha Agerich, Alfred Brendel and Murray Perahia. It is always a beautiful stay and then afterwards, one can continue eastwards to the fascinating walled city of **Carcasonne.** This amazing elevated historic city is one of the most visited in France...set so high up, it is quite unique.

Marseille: Of course this tremendously interesting Port city has been included on our journeys a couple of times. It is actually a city with two sides to it...the bustling port area (where 'la bouillabaise' originated.... the main restaurant associated with this great gourmet delight requires orders for the dish two days in advance!) and the upper principal part of the old city, with its cathedral, beautiful buildings, busy thoroughfares and always music performances of many kinds. Another attraction of Marseille is that it is a fairly close bus journey northwards to marvellous Aix-en Provence...and also the start of a beautiful train journey eastwards from there, along the coast to Cannes and Nice, with many delightful stopping off places in between.

COMPOSERS' HOUSES:

On several of our tours I have been able to include visits to some European composers' houses. The following fitted in well with plans during different years: LISZT; CHOPIN; BEETHOVEN; GRIEG; WAGNER; MOZART; MENDELLSOHN. On occasion I have been able to give short recitals for my groups in these lovely historic houses, where the composers' personal effects (often including their pianos) have been lovingly kept. Sometimes the actual historic pianos are there to see, but are off- limits for present day performance. In these cases (not always) there is usually an available grand piano in a Music Room at the house.

MOZART (1756-1797): VIENNA: The so called "Figaro House" in Schuberstrsse where the Mozart family spent two to three years was probably his happiest and most productive time. Unfortunately also the most expensive, and soon Mozart was forced to move his family elsewhere. A pretty residence on two floors and approached by cobbled streets, people love to visit here.

BEETHOVEN: (1770-1827): Vienna: Beethoven moved so many times, one lost count. But my groups and I have visited the lovely so called "Heiligenstadt House" just above the city on the edge of the Vienna Woods.(Famous also for the much written about 'Heiligenstadt Statement'). From here the master was easily able to take his long walks through the woods, so necessary for his contemplation. He was a great lover of Nature and so many of his opening musical phrases stemmed from these solitary contemplative walks.

LISZT: (1811-1886): WEIMAR: The "Hofgartener" at the edge of the extensive woods is beautiful, very simple and moving. This is where Liszt used to stay when he visited from Rome in his declining years.... so different to his earlier days in Weimar at the sumptuous "Altenburg", which we have also visited several times for concerts.

WAGNER: (1813-1883): LUZERN...this beautiful house called "Tribschen" overlooking the lake, where he and Cosima and children lived for several years. Notably, the house where he composed for Cosima, the "Siegfried Idyll". BAYREUTH: The absolutely sumptuous residence here, "Wahnfried" was provided by his patron, King Ludwig, with his own opera house nearby...the famous "Bayreuth Festspielhaus ". This interior, to my mind, is rather vulgar with over-the-top luxury.

CHOPIN: (1810-1849). We have visited his Paris apartment in the Rue de la Chausee d'Antin, and also where he lived at the end of his life...a ground floor apartment in the Place d'Orleans. Plus of course, on several occasions, the Chateau Nohant in the countryside 300 kms south of Paris, and about which I have written a considerable account of his years there with his lover, Aurore Dupin (George Sand).

MENDELSSOHN: (1809 – 1847). LEIPZIG: The Mendelssohns lived in several places (including Dresden) but we have visited the lovely residence in Leipzig several times, and where I have given a couple of short recitals for my groups. In an attractive block set in beautiful gardens, it is a quite large apartment on the second floor with a charming music room. I have also arranged a concert here with a trio who are members of the famous Gewandhaus Orchestra Leipzig. The striking thing for me here is the small study where this great composer worked.... seemingly standing at his desk. There are many family photos and one could sense the children running through the corridors and down to the gardens.

GRIEG: (1843-1907): BERGEN: Situated a little out of Bergen at Troldhaugen, this rustic and quite simple house was built for the young couple (Eduard and his wife, Nina) as a gift from the city of Bergen on the occasion of their silver wedding anniversary. Its interior follows the rustic theme with unpainted timber walls adorned by many framed photos and the large sitting room still contains Grieg's concert grand, on which I have been privileged to have played his "Wedding Day at Troldhaugen". The house sits on a green hill above the fjord and just below it is the timber cabin where this wonderful composer worked.

ELGAR: (1857-1934) There is so much more one could write about all the above houses of composers, but this is not the place to do so. I personally have visited a house of **ELGAR** and am disappointed not to have been able to include it in a tour. It is a simple cottage in Broadheath, Worcester, but as the composer became more famous, he and his family moved into larger places...but never far from this loved cottage in the Malvern Hills. One of our frequent LINGUA MUSICA tour members, and who also was the major figure in our "Wine and Music" tour, **Christopher Barnes AM**, actually has a connection with the Edward Elgar history. In 1904, Elgar bought the house,"Plas Gwyn"on the edge of Hereford from Chris's grandfather. He lived there till 1912 and it was here that his output was significant, including his First Symphony in 1908 and his Violin Concerto of 1910. Interestingly also is that the father of Christopher Barnes knew many of the people portrayed in Elgar's "Enigma Variations".

Deborah Tresise: Deborah is a busy Sydney lawyer. One of the very important things I have not mentioned so far is that in approximately 2006, my daughter, Deborah Tresise, created a website for LINGUA MUSICA. I would send her all the tour outlines and all my descriptions each year and Deborah would "put it up" (is that the expression?) on the website. This would be done very expertly and she would also find beautiful little coloured images to add for each location. I could never have done that. Am afraid my computer technical knowledge has always been confined to the very basics. The entries always looked so attractive. A thousand thanks to Deborah! She would then answer enquiries and send them on to me. When she had time away from her legal work, she would come on the tours as a very efficient and experienced Tour Assistant.

Deborah now has enormous experience and is in just the right position to take over, once this terrible pandemic has left us, and international travel becomes safe again.

Deborah's wonderful **"La Belle France 2020"** tour, with incredible French content and the ability for those pressed for time, to take in either one of two parts or as a whole, and which attracted so much interest, has of course been cancelled. Just like all international travel this year. We must hope that international borders will reopen around September 2021, and if not, then surely in 2022. And LINGUA MUSICA will again be able to offer the kind of detailed and personal travel people have come to expect of us.

"A SPANISH RHAPSODY"

It was **2017** and I had decided that this was to be my final LINGUA MUSICA European tour....my thirtieth! So it had to be a special one so far as the locations chosen within this very large southern country. So many people love Barcelona and that Mediterranean side of Spain. We had been there several times, as well as Valencia and beautiful places in between. But Barcelona, though absolutely wonderful in its own way, to my mind, has become too crowded with English tour groups in their red double-decker buses cramming the small streets and little cafes with signs offering "English Cream Teas" that I decided to give it a miss this time, and design a tour route travelling down the centre, from top to bottom and along the southern Costa del Sol. There was so much opportunity to include so much of great interest in this way. I also decided to do the entire tour with our own private bus, except for one magnificent and VERY FAST train trip between Madrid and Seville (not actually run by Thalys's...but perhaps owned by them. Very similar speed and first class service.)

The tour route that year, was Bilbao, San Sebastian, Madrid, Segovia, Seville, Cordoba, Cadiz, Granada, Marbella, Mijas. I wanted it to be a tour of very great contrasts and indeed it was.

There were a few personal little hiccups before this tour. Pre-tour, I had flown to Paris to visit some friends and on arrival, was conscious of not feeling as well as I might. Whilst walking around my favourite Latin Quarter region, had felt extremely breathless, rested a little here and there, then continued till suddenly overcome,had grasped an iron railing and felt not a little anxious. By chance, a young off-duty nurse, Ignazia de Caro, saw me and rushed to help. At her insistence, and to cut the story short, I found myself in an ambulance and then in the largest teaching hospital in Paris for two days. All fine, and continued on by train to stay with dear friends, Florence and Franck, (Florence had been involved in the very early tours) in pretty **St Jean-de-Luz** in the South West of France. Another rather strange episode called for a day with intensive tests at the very large and modern Hopitalier de la Cote Basque at Bayonne.(My poor patient dear friends! Fancy having to cope with all this!) Again all ok, but issued with some stern "warnings". Well, for heaven's sake, I had a group arriving BILBAO in two days' time and couldn't just abandon them at such short notice. Again, to cut a long story short, Florence and Franck drove me through the Basque country to Bilbao and we met as planned for the Welcome Lunch in the restaurant of our glamorous Hotel Grande Domine there. I was happy to see my group (including several annual ones) as well as my daughter, Deborah Tresise, who had flown up from Madrid the day before. All was well and we looked forward to a marvellously interesting tour. (I did allude very casually to my French experiences, playing it down, but advising I would not be taking part in any guided excursions. Apart from that, everything would be exactly as planned)....and it was. My excellent personally chosen Spanish organisers and guides with whom I had had very extended pre-tour communications were marvellous. Everything worked very well, and because I was always able to have those small 'time-out' periods, it was all most enjoyable.I opted out whenever I felt a bit overcome and everyone understood. All the while I was in communication with my dear friend, Bridget Buckley, CEO of a large group of language schools in Seville and who also had inherited the charming family Villa Sant Ana in **MIJAS**, about two hours south. My family and I had stayed during many years at this delightfully located villa perched in the mountains above the sea, and from whose terrace one could look out to Gibralta. We were to come up from our final stay in Marbella to finish our tour with drinks and the usual ham canapés (Ham is everywhere in Spain...in all its endless variety) on this terrace as guests of Bridget and husband, Andres, followed by a final lunch in a local typical village restaurant. MIJAS is just gorgeous and known as the most important of the famous "white-washed villages of Andalusia". (A strict regulation exists that owners must keep their properties regularly 'white-washed' and certainly, Villa Sant Ana was as white as one could imagine!). At the Villa, an enormous surprise had been arranged for me. Bridget's father, Dick Buckley, a retired medico from Kinsale, County Cork, Ireland, had flown out just to meet me here at the family villa where we had all holidayed once upon a time. We had not seen each other for years and it was so emotional we both shed some tears. I could hardly believe it. My dear friend, Nan, Dick's wife, had died some years before.

So here we were in **BILBAO.** And the chief reason to be here was the amazing **GUGGENHEIM MUSEUM** of Canadian born American architect Frank Gehry. Solomon Guggenheim had founded the Guggenheim Foundation in 1937 with a view to bringing to the public, the works of the great Kandinsky and his followers. It was Frank Lloyd Wright who designed the permanent Museum in New York. This was followed by the Peggy Guggenheim one in Venice, and now BILBAO. It is a most extraordinary building beside the River Nervion, and was officially opened by the former King Juan Carlos of Spain on October 18th 1997. It has been described as "a unique moment in architecture" and also as being "a fantastic dream ship sailing in a cloak of titanium". WELL! Words are words! Over the top descriptive ideas of enthusiasts. It is certainly captivating, but after a short lecture, and giving out all the notes, I felt it best to wander the incredible interior with all its fine exhibits, and allow my guests to form their own views as they did the same.. And it teemed with rain the entire time.

We in Australia have a rather close connection with Frank Gehry. I remember with delight being taken by my own architect son to visit his new University of Technology building in Sydney which had opened in 2015. I absolutely loved this incredible edifice with its facade of more than 320,000 hand-placed bricks (especially manufactured for the purpose) and held together by steel pins and glass slabs creating an undulating exterior. All this plus an arresting flow of beautiful interior spaces, lecture rooms and the stunning stainless steel stairways, giving the feeling of glass. I have always wanted to return. In fact, my thoughts returned to this beautiful example of Gehry's work as I strolled the Bilbao interiors and sheltered from the rains. Somehow or other, I found I much preferred the Sydney example of this brilliant man's work. Frank Gehry did several lectures and work in other parts of Australia. My son had had excellent and helpful conversations with him.

Onward to **SAN SEBASTIAN** and our HOTEL LONDRES beside the sea and almost on the sand. A beautiful city on the Bay of Biscay and only twenty Kms from the French border, it has a very long and involved history. It had actually been chosen by the European Community as the Cultural Capital 2016 and now in 2017, we could enjoy everything then arranged. Architechturally, it was during the 1860's that great emphasis was given to remodelling the city in the neo-classical style as well as including some dynamic modern buildings. The extraordinary KURSAAL PALACE with its many rooms for concerts and events designed by Spanish architect, Rafael Moneo, looks out over pounding surf and it is here that the famous film festival takes place. The HOTEL LONDRES has also known much history. Before its life as a hotel, it was the residence of Queen Isabella 11 who chose exile here when the Revolution triumphed. The tales of Isabella and also the young Asturian, Don Carlos, make interesting reading and have inspired many plays and also the Verdi opera, "Don Carlos". Some of the guests over the years included the French artist, Toulouse Lautrec, Archduchess Elizabeth of Austria, David Strauss, and the beautiful spy, MATA HARI! Now LINGUA MUSICA! Our 2017 group anticipated an interesting stay in the same place as Mata Hari, where a suite has been named after her. A beautiful concert in the main symphonic hall, several excellent restaurant meals above the sea, a guided evening tapas tour with our very lively local guide which they all adored, and as well a city one, made this visit to San Sebastian a most successful stay, despite on occasion, short but heavy rain falls.

MADRID: This absolutely wonderful capital city has been the subject of so much writing and study. It literally buzzes with life. A most beautifully laid out city with two major historic regions, it was all excellently shown and explained by our wonderful guide. Many walks, many rests, many coffee stops. The sun had returned in all its glory, but not too hot. (I sat it out, quite often resting at the tiny outdoor restaurant in the small square just outside our hotel, where they would all arrive later to tell me about their discoveries.) Madrid, and all over Spain, has lively and interesting gourmet attractions too. We loved our visits to all the chosen restaurants and cafes on the entire Spanish tour.

Apart from anything else (including a wonderful Mahler concert at the huge Nacional Auditorio de Musica, the opera, "Carmen", and an exciting flamenco display, there was so much history, which I wrote about for this group and the three great galleries, among the greatest in the world… **the Museo Nacional del Prado, the Museo Thyssen-Bormisza and the Centro de Arte Reina Sofia.** These magnificent galleries as well as the wonderful **PARC RETIRO** and Botanic Gardens are all situated in the central Golden Triangle, as it is known….all within walking distance of one another, and when tired out by all that art research, easy to rest out in the beautiful extensive park lands.

THE PRADO, so well known all over the world, contains the richest and most amazing paintings the world has seen. It takes four to five hours to tour the entire gallery at a comfortable walking pace, so decisions need to be made. And to make those decisions one needs to know the content and the layout. I made sure such decisions were made easier for my group by giving them so much printed information. The gallery was opened in 1819 and specialises in European art from the 12th – 19th centuries, actually reflecting the history of Spain, but with the greatest emphasis on the 16th/17th centuries. Diego Valesquez seems to have been the several monarchs' favourite and he naturally figures most prominently here.

I was able to give my guests a list of my own favourite works I had loved during several previous visits, even as far back as when we lived in England. But I left it to them, with the assistance of their guide, to make their own decisions. Mine were :

Fra Angelico: The Annunciation..1395. Raphael: Portrait of a

Cardinal..1510 Hieronymous Bosch: trypich....incl. the 'Garden of Earthly Delights'! Durer: Self Portrait 1498. Titan: Bachanalia 1519. Goya: Naked Maja 1797. Goya: Third of May 1808. Tintoretto: Christ washing disciples' feet. 1547. Velasquez: Triumph of Bachus 1629

And most favoured of all....Velasquez: **"Los Merimas"**, 1656.....just adore this work, the little princess and her beautifully detailed dress and hair, the mirror and its effect, and how realistic is that dog!!

The other two major galleries, **Thyssen-Bormisza**, (old masters and modern works) and the **Reina Sofia** were great attractions. The latter was named for Queen Sofia, wife of the former King Juan Carlos and mother of the present King Philipe V1. Sofia's Greek/German family was forced into exile during WW2. She is related to some of the British royals and has attended many British events like royal weddings and Wimbledon etc. She is absolutely passionate about the Arts including Music and works tirelessly in the field of child care. Queen Sofia speaks several languages and has been awarded a number of honorary degrees. Always beautifully dressed, she is a leader of fashion and intensely dislikes bullfights. It was she who worked so hard to have them banned in Spain.Twentieth Century Spanish Art is close to her heart and she was very involved in the foundation of this important gallery. It is here in fact that the most famous work of Pablo Picasso, the huge wall mural entitled **"Guernica"** can be seen.This was his immediate response to the hideous unnecessary Nazi bombing of small towns in Northern Spain, in particular one called Guernica.

SEGOVIA: A full day excursion to this historic capital of a region made up of Castile and Leon was led by our excellent guide and enjoyed by all. They visited the great Segovia Cathedral, the Alcazar (Royal Palace) and gardens and many other highlights of this beautiful city where some of the remnants of the ancient city walls, which were also aqueducts, are still visible and in fact are highlights of any visit here.

SEVILLE: For once giving our driver time off, we took the marvellous IVA fast two hour train trip from Madrid to Seville.This is a very special trip at great speed, with lunch served on trays just as on an airline. For me, one of the highlights of our stay in Seville was actually our hotel (one I had never used before but had been told so much about by a friend and former guest), the **Hotel Amadeus**, set in the old quarter. It is a work of art in itself. An 18th century former home of wealthy Sevillianos, ancient but absolutely immaculately kept and I was quite astonished by the amount of superbly polished silver in the several charmingly furnished sitting rooms, where a special secret hotel cocktail and small biscuits were frequently laid out for guests...a charming gesture. It is also very close to the famous Alcazar, Cathedral and Giralda and the surrounding narrow streets absolutely made for gentle walks. It is also a hotel which is very much about Music, displays very many musical instruments and hosts many chamber music concerts in its lovely music room. I actually gave a recital and short lecture of Spanish piano music there... works by Scarlatti, Albeniz, Granados and Mompou.

The guide in Seville, David Delgado, had become almost a friend during our very lengthy pre-tour conversations. He had arranged so much of great interest for the group and also had booked several wonderful restaurants, which I had not known, with special atmospheres and amazing food and wines. On the last day, he brought his new baby daughter to meet us at the hotel. Throughout our pre-tour conversations I had heard about this expected event in a few months and had brought her a special little dress from Melbourne.

CORDOBA :Naturally a day trip from Seville to CORDOBA was arranged and this UNESCO listed city is a most wonderful place to visit and to learn and finally understand how the Muslims, Jews and Christians had once all lived and worked successfully together before the so called Reconquista of the Catholic Church authorities. Cordoba in the very early days had been considered the leading city of learning in Europe because of its great advances in the fields of Science, Medicine, Architecture and Literature. After Ferdinand and Isabella came to the throne, everything changed. The city declined and this decline increased further after the Renaissance.

UNESCO today recognises the GREAT MOSQUE 0f CORDOBA as a world heritage site... (**"La Mezquita"**), the interior with its intricate amazing pillars and decorated ceilings is a sight to remember forever, and to wonder about how it once was, and sadly, how it might still have been.

In Seville we attended two excellent concerts, one by the Seville Symphony Orchestra at the Teatro Maestranza.

CADIZ: Almost all the group opted to take the optional day trip with David to CADIZ. I met a few who preferred to wander for coffee, and then caught up with some old friends who live in Seville for lunch plus a matinee concert. CADIZ is one of the oldest cities in Spain and the main port of the Navy since the 18thc takeover by the Spanish Bourbons. Prettily located by the sea, it has many attractions David promised to show them with time for a seaside wander after a Cadiz-style gourmet lunch.

GRANADA: Goodness what a place this is! What intensity here! How full of different pieces of fascinating history! How amazingly laid out, with the famous Alhambra Palace at the top! After its very very earliest history, the first actual council of Granada was held in 306 AD. As elsewhere, the Muslims took over and great knowledge and research was continued here till 1492, when Ferdinand and Isabella over-ruled them.Things turned very badly indeed for the poor Muslims and Jews, though some of the Moors, one has to say, did very well. The Generaliffe Palace and Estate were the summer residence of the Nastrid rulers.... the gardens here are the oldest surviving Moorish ones in Spain.But not everything was too bad for the inhabitants. Columbus was given permission to go off looking for a new world, and of course discovered the Americas. Splendour gradually increased in Granada, with beautiful Gothic architecture and a concentration on Art and Music. Many years later, Manuel de Falla was the leading composer here and the great Auditorio is named for him. Granada is so well known throughout the world...so unique in every way. UNESCO has declared both the Alhambra Palace and the Generaliffe Gardens to be world heritage sites.

The groups always enjoyed Granada to the full, with guided excursions, beautiful meals on the terrace of the glamorous Alhambra Palace Hotel where we stayed, and in 2017, a wonderful classical guitar recital there by the then leading guitar recitalist in Spain, Maestro Jose Manuel

Canol Robles. Not only a brilliant and widely travelled musician, but a delightful person. He joined the group for dinner as my guest and had lively conversation in Spanish with Caroline. I think because of the maestro's distinguished presence, the Manager of the Hotel Alhambra Palace also joined us for dinner. So the conversation in Spanish and English was well managed.

MARBELLA: A rather long trip in our private bus took us along the coast and above remote villages to MARBELLA, one of the smartest resorts in Europe. This was designed as a "holiday at the tour's end ". Our location was an 'apartment/hotel' right on the sea, each with its own kitchen and terrace and also a beautiful dining room at ground level. It was a short step to the wide promenade by the sea, where fashionably dressed holiday makers strolled to find one of the many little restaurants of all kinds. A couple of the less experienced members of our group had not realised the nature of an apartment/hotel and at first were a little flummoxed. But they soon caught on and enjoyed our Recovery three days here. There was actually a lot to enjoy, and one needed also to explore the old town whose history goes back to 1600 BC. The acclaimed British writer,Laurie Lee (**"As I walked out one summer morning "**) tells of his walk from the north to south of Spain and the fate of this region here during the terrible Spanish Civil War. Marbella is now a glamorous and popular resort (thanks to several canny Irish businessmen who saw its potential in the mid-forties) but it does also have this long and often unhappy history.

MIJAS: Up in the nearby mountains above Marbella there is this little gem, MIJAS. (pronounced Mee-haas).Only about 40 minutes winding drive up, the tiny village is full of books, art and craft and many restaurants. It's famous as the most important of the so called "White Villages of Anadalusia". As I have said earlier, the strict regulations here demand that property owners keep their places well white- washed at all times, and amid all the greenery and colourful flowers this white stone creates a beautiful ambience. Our friends' villa,Villa Sant Ana, is quite historic and from its terrace, one can look out over the large pool and blue sea as far as Gibralta. My family and I had spent many happy times there and today we were to be guests for champers and canapés before our Farewell Lunch in a very lively, very typical Mijas Village restaurant. It was a very happy occasion.

We returned to Marbella for final packing and final walks along the Promenade before waving goodbye to them all next morning as they took off in our private van for Malaga Airport some 40 minutes away.

That day was October 1st, 2017, and was the birthday of daughter and Tour Assistant, Deborah Tresise. Deborah's daughter (and my eldest grandchild) Caroline, had flown in from Seville. She had joined in a little with the group in the final couple of days but was working desperately hard to complete the writing up of her first master's thesis and had not come to Mijas the day before. September 30th, and October 1st had seen her barely move from her desk. Finally done! And the helpful Reception staff printed it all for her and sent it off to Rome! She was free at last. I remember a leisurely walk along the Promenade and a lovely birthday dinner around a white clothed table with beautifully polished glass and silver at a splendidly located Italian outdoor restaurant right beside the waves. A beautiful birthday dinner and a beautiful end to a magnificent tour… actually the last. My final LINGUA MUSICA European tour! It was both a happy and nostalgic occasion and I was glad to be spending it with these two much loved people who had for years been so involved in those same tours. "Happy Days!"

CONCLUSION

What can I say? The seven/eight months of isolation during this Melbourne Covid lockdown have been extremely challenging for me as also for so many others. It has tested one's resilience and one's imagination. It has been very interesting to hear and to read of the many ways in which different Melburnians responded, many finding an ability to be creative.

For me, it was not all negativity. There were many positive aspects to this isolation too. It gave me time to do more practice and time to listen to more music. Listening became more important to me than ever. ABC Classic FM became even more appreciated than ever before...often in my car above the sea. The beauty of Nature, the sea, the coastal vegetation along the cliff paths, the birds, the tiny children with enormous helmets on tiny scooters and bikes...all tugged at my heart and filled me with ever increasing gratitude and joy. And that precious time...that previously elusive element, time, was such a wonderful gift. Time for reflection, time to check more frequently on family and friends, and time for memories. So many wonderful memories! Of travel and other experiences with my husband and children. And also the memories I revisited from rereading my tour Handbooks and personal diaries truly amazed me. The inevitable result of all these has been this memoir and written account of thirty years of LINGUA MUSICA European Music and Art tours. It has been a rewarding journey for me. And I do hope it may be of some interest to others who enjoy cultural travel and the opportunity to experience great music, great art, and great discoveries.

It is now December 2020, and here in Melbourne, we are finally and cautiously moving outwards. Cautiously yes. But one may now begin to hope that the reopening of international borders will no longer appear to be so impossible to imagine. And perhaps also LINGUA MUSICA will again be able to offer the kind of special experiences and personal attention our participants have come to expect.

There is a definite elation in the air...a real sense of gratitude...and a sense of hope. We are so fortunate in Australia. But Europe will continue to beckon. Could we possibly hope for 2022 I wonder?

ACKNOWLEDGEMENTS

First and foremost, my enormous thanks go to all those wonderful participants, who, over so many years, have trusted me to provide for them the kind of tours I had described. This trust has been of enormous significance and has enabled me to continue to create so many continuing and very different LINGUA MUSICA adventures.

I am enormously grateful also to my daughters and eldest granddaughter, Deborah, Jackie and Caroline, who were wonderfully supportive and very efficient in their Assistant roles and also very knowledgeable and able in their professional input on many occasions. I also acknowledge the great input of dear friend, the late Clive Stark, as a wonderful Tour Escort for many years.

To Ruth Nye, my love and enormous thanks for her wonderful contributions on several tours. Her great musical input, her lectures, as well as her charming serene personality were always captivating for my groups.

To Terry Lewis, love and thanks for all those remarkable situations when your practical support and management saved the day. And for your own professional input which was always marvellous.

To all those wonderful performers (sometimes friends), my deep admiration and appreciation of your great gifts. And to all the European friends who contributed to the success of these tours, my enormous thanks. I also have great appreciation of all the marvellous European guides over so many years and in so many different countries.

To my professional and expert travel agents, Anne O'Brien and later Brenna Jones, my very sincere thanks for your help and advice.

ACKNOWLEDGEMENTS

To all those innumerable European agents with whom I worked, my great appreciation.

To all those involved in making each tour a success, even if not possible to recognise individually, my very sincere thanks.

My deepest thanks to my designer, Luke Harris. His patience, his practicality, his many skills, and his kindness are what finally turned my sometimes confused remembrances into a coherent memoir. Could never have happened without you, Luke.

And finally, to my dear family…much love and thanks for supporting and encouraging me for so many years and for putting up with me when at times the frantic efforts to get everything completed almost overwhelmed me.

www.ingramcontent.com/pod-product-compliance
Lightning Source LLC
Chambersburg PA
CBHW062034290426
44109CB00026B/2623